BUTTERFLY SZN

A guided journal that uses heartwork to transmute your suffering in cocoon season into an empowered butterfly butterfly season.

….because afterall, the beauty is in the transformation.

AISHA MARSHALL

JOIN THE MOVEMENT, BE THE CHANGE.

When you pick up the Butterfly SZN journal, you're not just buying a book; you're fueling a dream that goes way beyond us. You're supporting a collective healing.

Got a moment from your Butterfly SZN journey you wanna share? Post it on TikTok or Instagram, and we'll hook you up with **25% off your next purchase.**

Just DM @itsbutterflyszn us or shoot over an email to info@butterflyszn. com with your post link, and let's keep this high vibe spreading. Your story is a big part of this bigger picture we're all painting.

COMMITMENT TO TRANSFORMATION

I,———————————————————, am ready to step into into my transformation. Today, I'm saying 'yes' to navigating through my own seasons—from the exploration of caterpillar season, diving deep in the reflection of my cocoon season, to living in my power during my butterfly season. With each page I fill, I'm diving into a journey of self-discovery, committed to embracing my healing and transformation.

———————————————————

SIGNATURE

———————————————————

START DATE

———————————————————

COMPLETION DATE

TABLE OF CONTENTS

INTRODUCTION-- ix

CHAPTER 1: THE ALCHEMY OF TRANSFORMATION---------- 1

CHAPTER 2: THE SEASONS --- 3

CHAPTER 3: HEARTWORK -- 7

CHAPTER 4: THE SEED OF THE SOUL --------------------------- 9

CHAPTER 5: GERMINATION-------------------------------------69

CHAPTER 6: DISCOVERING YOUR COPING MECHANISMS --89

CHAPTER 7: SPROUTING ------------------------------------- 123

CHAPTER 8: BREAKING THE CYLE-------------------------- 155

CHAPTER 9: REPLANTING -------------------------------------- 159

CHAPTER 10: FLOWERING------------------------------------- 195

CHAPTER 11: BUTTERFLY SEASON -------------------------- 227

PREFACE

Welcome to the beginning of a unique journey. This isn't just a book; it's your doorway to a new kind of freedom, the kind you've been seeking. This journey is about breaking free from whatever's been weighing you down and sparking a change that goes beyond just you.

I wrote this book with a dream in mind. I want you to grow, but I also want your growth to mean something for everyone, for the collective. Through diving deep into my struggles, I've found ways to help others escape theirs. So now I want to pass that on to you. I want to empower you to create the life you've always wanted.

So, as you do this book's *heartwork*, remember, you're not just working on yourself; you're contributing to the bigger picture. Every insight, every breakthrough, and every new habit is a piece of a much larger puzzle. By becoming the change you need, you are becoming the change that the world needs.

Here's to you, your journey ahead, and the incredible things you can achieve when you decide to free yourself and light the way for others. Are you ready to start that ripple? Welcome to your Butterfly Season.

ACKNOWLEDGEMENT

This book is a testament to the power of personal transformation and the collective spirit that drives us to support one another on our journeys. I want to extend my deepest gratitude to the incredible people who have contributed to making this book a reality, to my family and friends for their endless love and encouragement, to my mentors and peers for their wisdom and guidance, and to my team for their dedication and hard work; and to you, dear reader, for your courage and commitment to growth. So, before we dive into the heart of our work together, let us take a moment to acknowledge and thank those who have helped and guided me through bringing these pages to life.

Cameron Marshall

Rebecca Alcaraz

Julia Reyder

Lizy Hoeffer

Kelly Kussman

Alexandra Zaki

Sam Harper

Paige Sterling

Jake Kelfer

Janay Douglas

Jamil Douglas

Eli Alcaraz

Sara Silver

Nikki Butler

Lauren Boyd

INTRODUCTION

On these pages lies a promise: to guide you from the shadows of cocoon season into the gift of your butterfly season, transforming your suffering into empowerment with every heartwork exercise. Butterfly SZN comes after the storm. It is the fruit of your labor, a celebration of transformation and renewal.

However, before butterfly season arrives, there is the cocoon season, a phase filled with trials and tribulations. The problem many of us face is the suffering in our cocoon season. It keeps us trapped in a loop of false starts, delays, and repeated issues that intensify with each cycle. While these challenges help us build the tools necessary for growth, they often require some insight to reveal how we can get out of our own way and onto our desired life path.

I was in that loop for three years, meeting the same types of people, going through the same kind of relationship drama, facing the same life problems, and feeling stuck, year after year. It felt like an invisible hand was holding me back, stopping me from moving forward. I was exhausted and fed up with where life was heading. I was frustrated by the stagnation until I realized that the only direction left to explore was inward.

That's when things started to change. Deep-diving into myself during therapy, I stumbled upon something outstanding: the power of asking the right questions. It's incredible how the right questions unearth crucial information inside us. Through self-exploration, I realized I was the invisible hand holding me back.

My experience inspired this journal. I thought, "If asking the right questions helped me break free from my loops, why can't I use the same line of questioning every time I feel stuck?" Or even better, it could do the same for others. So here it is, a tool to guide you through your journey of self-discovery and healing through the power of introspection and asking the right questions.

With this journal, you embark on a journey of transmuting self-imposed suffering, suffering that persists unbeknownst to its creator. The core of this journal is about engaging in heartwork: a process of introspection and emotional unearthing to reveal and address the most profound parts of yourself. By doing the heartwork, you can connect with your emotions, understand your unmet needs, and empower yourself to take deliberate actions to heal and grow. Heartwork uses the wisdom of your heart to navigate life's challenges and transform your suffering into strength.

Think of this journal as your cocoon, a safe space for introspection leading to metamorphosis. You will explore the depths of your emotions, confront events that have shaped you, and nurture your unmet needs through guided prompts. As you progress, you'll find your wings and emerge stronger, wiser, and ready to soar.

The Butterfly SZN journal mirrors a caterpillar's natural progression as it morphs into a butterfly. Your unique journey is segmented into exercises that reflect each growth stage: starting as a caterpillar, moving into the cocoon phase, and finally emerging in the butterfly season. Each exercise is thoughtfully crafted to align with these stages and facilitate your personal growth and metamorphosis. As you venture into the heart of the journal, you begin the heartwork exercises, where deep introspection and emotional exploration occur. There, you'll engage in activities to bring your innermost feelings, challenges, and aspirations to the surface, setting the stage for your profound transformation.

Thank you for trusting me to guide you on your journey. The Butterfly SZN journal is a companion through any life stage, offering structured but flexible pathways to self-awareness and renewal. So, embrace your season of transformation with courage and hope. Remember, every significant change begins with a single, brave step. Let the Butterfly SZN Journal and our community support you as you spread your wings and soar into the life you were meant to live. Together, we share insights, celebrate progress, and support each other through the challenges and triumphs of our metamorphoses.

For a deeper dive into the themes of transformation and self-discovery, I invite you to tune into The Butterfly SZN Podcast, which is available on all streaming platforms. Every episode complements your journey with stories, interviews, and tips illuminating your evolutionary path.

For daily doses of inspiration and connection, follow us on Instagram at @itsbutterflyszn. There, you'll find a community eager to embrace you, share experiences, and offer encouragement as you spread your wings.

Thank you for trusting the Butterfly SZN Journal with your most profound fears, hopes, and dreams. Together, we'll explore the beauty of transformation and the power of heartwork. Here's to finding your wings and soaring into your best season yet.

CHAPTER 1

THE ALCHEMY OF TRANSFORMATION

Navigating from suffering to freedom through heartwork is a beautiful and transformative journey. The profound and introspective work you'll do with this journal bridges your inner turmoil with the wisdom to move forward. As you dive into your heartwork, you'll find it naturally inspires action informed by the insights and understanding you've gained. Your progression from suffering to freedom and action captures the essence of transmuting suffering energy into empowerment. That transformation, facilitated by heartwork, harnesses the power to shift your perception of challenges and responses to them, turning your most challenging struggles into your greatest strengths.

Suffering, while challenging, is a catalyst for personal growth, opening doors to a more profound understanding of ourselves. By engaging with this journal, you will step through that door, where exploring your innermost shadows, the lowest frequencies of human behavior, reveals the wisdom within your suffering. That wisdom, uncovered through doing the heartwork exercises, lights your path to transformation and arms you with the tools for personal change.

Wisdom emerges as you engage with the heartwork, sorting through your experiences with a fine-tooth comb and finding the truth to light your way forward. Decision-making guided by this wisdom goes beyond quick fixes; it provides a profound understanding of the roots of your problems and helps you comprehend your underlying motivations. By understanding the foundation, you're equipped to recognize the drivers behind your old actions. Then, as similar situations emerge, your insights allow you to address those drivers at their source so that you can choose new actions aligned with your goals and true to your core values. This approach encourages you to break free from your cyclical patterns. It sets you up for a life of intention, peace, and genuine alignment.

Turning your suffering into wisdom grants you the power to take control of your life, initiating a transformative journey that begins with recognizing the patterns and sources of your suffering. Heartwork is crucial to this process. It offers a fresh perspective to empower you to change from viewing yourself as a victim to becoming the author of your life story, including narratives previously hidden from your awareness.

With this newfound awareness, action naturally follows. The heartwork within this journal is a catalyst, deepening your connection to your emotions and highlighting your unmet needs. This empowers you to take deliberate steps toward healing and growth, transform your profound fears and suffering, and lay the groundwork for enduring transformation and fulfillment.

CHAPTER 2

THE SEASONS

The Butterfly SZN journal is structured around the metaphorical journey of personal transformation, mirroring the life stages of a butterfly. This journey is divided into three distinct "seasons," each representing a growth and self-discovery phase. Let's dive into them.

Caterpillar Season: Unawareness to Awareness

Caterpillar Season focuses on moving from a state of unawareness to awareness. This phase is about recognizing patterns, behaviors, and beliefs that have been operating beneath the surface of your consciousness. Like a caterpillar, which begins its life journey unaware of its potential to fly, you start by exploring the aspects of your life you have never questioned or noticed. The exercises encourage you to reflect on your current state, identify areas for growth, and become more mindful of your thoughts, feelings, and actions. Your awareness is the first step toward transformation.

Cocoon Season: Unlearn to Relearn

Cocoon Season is a time for introspection and deep inner work. The focus shifts from unlearning outdated or limiting beliefs to relearning and embracing empowering truths. It's an in-between period where you are no longer a caterpillar but still not a butterfly. This season is characterized by reflection, healing, and the challenging but necessary step of releasing what no longer serves you. This phase's exercises help you dig deep into your inner world, confront uncomfortable truths, and construct a framework for understanding yourself and the world around you.

Butterfly Season: Empowerment to Action

Butterfly Season is the culmination of your journey, where empowerment becomes action. Having become aware and redefined your beliefs and values, you're ready to spread your wings and put your newfound understanding into practice. This season is about embodying the change you've worked toward, living your truth, and taking decisive steps toward your goals and dreams. This phase's exercises motivate and guide concrete actions that reflect your growth, empowerment, and the life you're creating for yourself. It's a time of celebration, achievement, and living with purpose, fully embracing the beauty of your transformation.

Each season in the Butterfly SZN journal is a structured yet flexible path toward personal evolution, reflecting the natural and beautiful process of becoming who you are meant to be.

Life's Multifaceted Seasons

Life doesn't neatly compartmentalize into single transformative seasons. Instead, it embraces the complexity and synchronicity of various seasons across many life aspects. You could be in a financial Butterfly Season, thriving and making empowered decisions, while navigating a relationship Cocoon Season full of introspection and reevaluation. Similarly, you could be in a professional life Caterpillar Season, discovering new potentials and awareness, even as you enter a health and fitness Cocoon Season, shedding poor habits while fostering healthier ones.

Understanding the distinctions between the different aspects of your life is crucial to applying them to your journey. You can become resilient by recognizing where you are in each area of your life and adapting your approach to change accordingly. Your nuanced awareness will allow you to identify your specific patterns and challenges unique to each season and life aspect. The more precisely you can pinpoint your current season concerning each aspect of your life, the more effectively you can address and transform your patterns.

If you're unsure which season you may be in, let our quiz be the first step to steering your thoughts and intentions inward. It will reveal the general theme of your life's current season and spark curiosity about the work ahead. Approach the quiz with an open heart and mind, allowing it to challenge and expand your perspectives. The quiz is more than a preliminary step; think of it as a warm-up, preparing you mentally and emotionally for the following heartwork. You can take the quiz at www.butterflyszn.com/quiz.

YOUR
DIRECTION
IS MORE
IMPORTANT
THAN YOUR
SPEED.

BUTTERFLY SZN

CHAPTER 3

HEARTWORK

L et's address the elephant in the room: heartwork. What is heartwork? This book's heartwork consists of reflective exercises that challenge you to explore your feelings, understand your patterns, and, ultimately, cultivate a deeper connection with yourself. As you do these exercises, you'll learn to embrace your journey with kindness and curiosity, allowing each discovery to guide you toward intentional living.

It's important to remember that heartwork is not linear. There will be days when the intensity of the work feels overwhelming. When that happens, it's okay to pause and breathe. You can revisit the Butterfly SZN Journal whenever you are ready. Treat it like a constant companion as you weave through the ebbs and flows of your personal growth. When you find the value in this journal, please consider sharing your experience by gifting a copy to a friend or relative.

IF I AM
HOLDING BACK ON
MY POTENTIAL,
IT IS MY
RESPONSIBILITY
TO FIGURE OUT HOW
TO GET OUT OF MY
OWN WAY.

BUTTERFLY SZN

CHAPTER 4

THE SEED OF THE SOUL

We start at the root, the seed of the soul. This chapter helps you move from not knowing what's happening inside you to getting a clear picture. Think of it as when you begin noticing patterns that keep popping up over and over again, the moments that make you think, "Why does this keep happening to me?"

This chapter's heartwork exercises will help you spot the issues and allow the repeated patterns to point to the essence of your inner self that's been waiting for you to notice it.

As you dive in, think of it as an opportunity to bring awareness to the seed you didn't plant yourself but has been quietly shaping you from the shadows. You'll give this seed the spotlight it hasn't had before and begin to understand how it has woven itself into the fabric of who you are.

WE HAVE BECOME
SO USED TO SEEING
THE END RESULT
OF PEOPLE WINNING
MATERIALISTICALLY
THAT WE HAVE
NO IDEA WINNING
SPIRITUALLY
PRECEDES IT.

BUTTERFLY SZN

CATERPILLAR SEASON

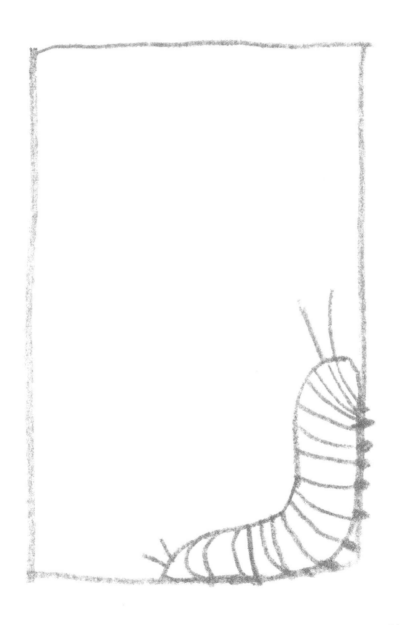

YOU WILL
TRANSFORM
IN WAYS YOU
NEVER THOUGHT
POSSIBLE

BUTTERFLY SZN

HEART

~~HOME~~ WORK EXERCISE 1

HEARTWORK EXERCISE 1: THE ISSUE

Please take a moment to settle into a comfortable space where your thoughts can flow freely. As you prepare to write, remember that this is a journey of self-discovery, not judgment. Hold your pencil lightly, and let it move as freely as your thoughts. At this stage, there's no need to worry about organization or clarity; your goal is simply to explore and express.

Look back at times when things didn't go as you had planned or you were disappointed with the outcome.

You don't have to be elaborate. The only thing that matters is that you understand your own words.

Simply list times when you intended one thing to happen, but something else happened instead, and events when you were frustrated by the outcome?

The exercise is to help you reflect on events in your life that are trying to surface. Simply state what happened and why you were disappointed.

At this point, you don't need to look for a theme or pattern of events. Those will emerge as you work through the exercises.

TIP: *Reflect on your experiences without filtering or holding back. Allow your writing to capture the events and the feelings and thoughts that emerged from them. Understanding often comes from simply allowing yourself to remember and acknowledge your experiences. Remember, there's no right or wrong way to do this; just let your pencil flow and your heart speak.*

THE SITUATION

WHO WAS INVOLVED?

WHAT HAPPENED THAT YOU DIDN'T PLAN FOR?

HEARTWORK EXERCISE 1: THE ISSUE

TIP: *Reflect on your experiences without filtering or holding back. Allow your writing to capture the events and the feelings and thoughts that emerged from them. Understanding often comes from simply allowing yourself to remember and acknowledge your experiences. Remember, there's no right or wrong way to do this; just let your pencil flow and your heart speak.*

THE SITUATION

WHO WAS INVOLVED?

WHAT HAPPENED THAT YOU DIDN'T PLAN FOR?

HEARTWORK EXERCISE 1: THE ISSUE

TIP: *Reflect on your experiences without filtering or holding back. Allow your writing to capture the events and the feelings and thoughts that emerged from them. Understanding often comes from simply allowing yourself to remember and acknowledge your experiences. Remember, there's no right or wrong way to do this; just let your pencil flow and your heart speak.*

THE SITUATION

WHO WAS INVOLVED?

WHAT HAPPENED THAT
YOU DIDN'T PLAN FOR?

HEARTWORK EXERCISE 1: THE ISSUE

TIP: *Reflect on your experiences without filtering or holding back. Allow your writing to capture the events and the feelings and thoughts that emerged from them. Understanding often comes from simply allowing yourself to remember and acknowledge your experiences. Remember, there's no right or wrong way to do this; just let your pencil flow and your heart speak.*

THE SITUATION

WHO WAS INVOLVED?

WHAT HAPPENED THAT YOU DIDN'T PLAN FOR?

HEARTWORK EXERCISE 1: THE ISSUE

TIP: *Reflect on your experiences without filtering or holding back. Allow your writing to capture the events and the feelings and thoughts that emerged from them. Understanding often comes from simply allowing yourself to remember and acknowledge your experiences. Remember, there's no right or wrong way to do this; just let your pencil flow and your heart speak.*

THE SITUATION

WHO WAS INVOLVED?

WHAT HAPPENED THAT YOU DIDN'T PLAN FOR?

HEARTWORK EXERCISE 1: THE ISSUE

TIP: Reflect on your experiences without filtering or holding back. Allow your writing to capture the events and the feelings and thoughts that emerged from them. Understanding often comes from simply allowing yourself to remember and acknowledge your experiences. Remember, there's no right or wrong way to do this; just let your pencil flow and your heart speak.

THE SITUATION

WHO WAS INVOLVED?

WHAT HAPPENED THAT
YOU DIDN'T PLAN FOR?

HEARTWORK EXERCISE 1: THE ISSUE

TIP: Reflect on your experiences without filtering or holding back. Allow your writing to capture the events and the feelings and thoughts that emerged from them. Understanding often comes from simply allowing yourself to remember and acknowledge your experiences. Remember, there's no right or wrong way to do this; just let your pencil flow and your heart speak.

THE SITUATION

WHO WAS INVOLVED?

WHAT HAPPENED THAT
YOU DIDN'T PLAN FOR?

HEARTWORK EXERCISE 1: THE ISSUE

TIP: *Reflect on your experiences without filtering or holding back. Allow your writing to capture the events and the feelings and thoughts that emerged from them. Understanding often comes from simply allowing yourself to remember and acknowledge your experiences. Remember, there's no right or wrong way to do this; just let your pencil flow and your heart speak.*

THE SITUATION

WHO WAS INVOLVED?

WHAT HAPPENED THAT YOU DIDN'T PLAN FOR?

HEARTWORK EXERCISE 1: THE ISSUE

TIP: *Reflect on your experiences without filtering or holding back. Allow your writing to capture the events and the feelings and thoughts that emerged from them. Understanding often comes from simply allowing yourself to remember and acknowledge your experiences. Remember, there's no right or wrong way to do this; just let your pencil flow and your heart speak.*

THE SITUATION

WHO WAS INVOLVED?

WHAT HAPPENED THAT YOU DIDN'T PLAN FOR?

HEARTWORK EXERCISE 1: THE ISSUE

TIP: *Reflect on your experiences without filtering or holding back. Allow your writing to capture the events and the feelings and thoughts that emerged from them. Understanding often comes from simply allowing yourself to remember and acknowledge your experiences. Remember, there's no right or wrong way to do this; just let your pencil flow and your heart speak.*

THE SITUATION

WHO WAS INVOLVED?

WHAT HAPPENED THAT YOU DIDN'T PLAN FOR?

HEARTWORK EXERCISE 1: THE ISSUE

TIP: *Reflect on your experiences without filtering or holding back. Allow your writing to capture the events and the feelings and thoughts that emerged from them. Understanding often comes from simply allowing yourself to remember and acknowledge your experiences. Remember, there's no right or wrong way to do this; just let your pencil flow and your heart speak.*

THE SITUATION

WHO WAS INVOLVED?

WHAT HAPPENED THAT YOU DIDN'T PLAN FOR?

HEARTWORK EXERCISE 1: THE ISSUE

TIP: Reflect on your experiences without filtering or holding back. Allow your writing to capture the events and the feelings and thoughts that emerged from them. Understanding often comes from simply allowing yourself to remember and acknowledge your experiences. Remember, there's no right or wrong way to do this; just let your pencil flow and your heart speak.

THE SITUATION

WHO WAS INVOLVED?

WHAT HAPPENED THAT YOU DIDN'T PLAN FOR?

HEART ~~HOME~~ WORK EXERCISE 2

HEARTWORK EXERCISE 2: THE EMOTIONS

This exercise aims to dive deep into the emotions tied to the experiences you've been exploring. As you work through your memories, you might find a particular event or recurring theme that stands out. It may feel as if your mind is gently nudging you and hinting that these areas might benefit from you taking a closer look at them. Please remember that you only need to focus on your feelings in this exercise.

Step 1: Identify Your Feelings Using the Emotion Wheel

The Emotion Wheel is a powerful tool to help you articulate and understand your feelings more precisely. The wheel breaks complex emotions into core (or "parent") feelings, making it easier to see the root of your emotional responses. Use the Emotion Wheel (below) to identify how the event made you feel. Note those emotions in the corresponding "Feelings" category.

Step 2: Connect Your Feelings to Parent Feelings

In the "Parent Feeling" column, link the feelings you identified to their corresponding parent feeling on the Emotion Wheel. The parent feelings are broader categories under which your specific emotional responses fall. They will provide a clearer understanding of your emotional landscape. Understanding the "parent" or core feelings is crucial because that understanding lays the groundwork for the more profound emotional work ahead.

Step 3: Fill In The Columns

Use what you've learned so far to fill in the columns underneath the Emotion Wheel:

- ❒ Name the situation: give a name to the events you identified in Heartwork Exercise One.

- ❒ Who was involved: Name the other people involved (if any) in the column beside the situation.

- ❒ What happened: In the following column, summarize the events.

- ❒ Feelings: Use the Emotion Wheel to help you identify every feeling that arises when you think about how the event that didn't turn out as you hoped.

- ❒ Parent Feeling: Use the Emotion Wheel to find the corresponding *parent* (or core) feeling you listed in the 'Feelings' column.

Please remember this exercise is not about finding immediate solutions or judging your experiences. It's about gaining a deeper, fuller understanding of how those experiences shaped your emotional world. Understanding your emotions and what provoked them will be instrumental as you move forward. They will help you to navigate your feelings and reactions with greater awareness and intention.

TIP: Once you've identified a situation that didn't turn out as you had hoped, take a deep breath. Afterward, describe the situation and note who else (if anyone) was involved. Then, write down how the situation made you feel. What thoughts and emotions arise as you revisit the memory? How did it make you feel? Use the emotion wheel to find the most appropriate name for your feelings.

EMOTION WHEEL

HEARTWORK EXERCISE 2: THE EMOTIONS

TIP: *Once you've identified a situation that didn't turn out as you had hoped, take a deep breath. Afterward, describe the situation and note who else (if anyone) was involved. Then, write down how the situation made you feel. What thoughts and emotions arise as you revisit the memory? How did it make you feel? Use the emotion wheel to find the most appropriate name for your feelings.*

GIVE THE SITUATION A NAME

WHO WAS INVOLVED?

WHAT HAPPENED?

FEELINGS

PARENT FEELINGS

HEARTWORK EXERCISE 2: THE EMOTIONS

TIP: *Once you've identified a situation that didn't turn out as you had hoped, take a deep breath. Afterward, describe the situation and note who else (if anyone) was involved. Then, write down how the situation made you feel. What thoughts and emotions arise as you revisit the memory? How did it make you feel? Use the emotion wheel to find the most appropriate name for your feelings.*

GIVE THE SITUATION A NAME

WHO WAS INVOLVED?

WHAT HAPPENED?

FEELINGS

PARENT FEELINGS

HEARTWORK EXERCISE 2: THE EMOTIONS

TIP: *Once you've identified a situation that didn't turn out as you had hoped, take a deep breath. Afterward, describe the situation and note who else (if anyone) was involved. Then, write down how the situation made you feel. What thoughts and emotions arise as you revisit the memory? How did it make you feel? Use the emotion wheel to find the most appropriate name for your feelings.*

HEARTWORK EXERCISE 2: THE EMOTIONS

TIP: *Once you've identified a situation that didn't turn out as you had hoped, take a deep breath. Afterward, describe the situation and note who else (if anyone) was involved. Then, write down how the situation made you feel. What thoughts and emotions arise as you revisit the memory? How did it make you feel? Use the emotion wheel to find the most appropriate name for your feelings.*

HEARTWORK EXERCISE 2: THE EMOTIONS

TIP: *Once you've identified a situation that didn't turn out as you had hoped, take a deep breath. Afterward, describe the situation and note who else (if anyone) was involved. Then, write down how the situation made you feel. What thoughts and emotions arise as you revisit the memory? How did it make you feel? Use the emotion wheel to find the most appropriate name for your feelings.*

GIVE THE SITUATION
A NAME

WHO WAS INVOLVED?

WHAT HAPPENED?

FEELINGS

PARENT FEELINGS

HEARTWORK EXERCISE 2: THE EMOTIONS

TIP: *Once you've identified a situation that didn't turn out as you had hoped, take a deep breath. Afterward, describe the situation and note who else (if anyone) was involved. Then, write down how the situation made you feel. What thoughts and emotions arise as you revisit the memory? How did it make you feel? Use the emotion wheel to find the most appropriate name for your feelings.*

GIVE THE SITUATION A NAME

WHO WAS INVOLVED?

WHAT HAPPENED?

FEELINGS

PARENT FEELINGS

HEARTWORK EXERCISE 2: THE EMOTIONS

TIP: *Once you've identified a situation that didn't turn out as you had hoped, take a deep breath. Afterward, describe the situation and note who else (if anyone) was involved. Then, write down how the situation made you feel. What thoughts and emotions arise as you revisit the memory? How did it make you feel? Use the emotion wheel to find the most appropriate name for your feelings.*

GIVE THE SITUATION
A NAME

WHO WAS INVOLVED?

WHAT HAPPENED?

FEELINGS

PARENT FEELINGS

HEARTWORK EXERCISE 2: THE EMOTIONS

TIP: *Once you've identified a situation that didn't turn out as you had hoped, take a deep breath. Afterward, describe the situation and note who else (if anyone) was involved. Then, write down how the situation made you feel. What thoughts and emotions arise as you revisit the memory? How did it make you feel? Use the emotion wheel to find the most appropriate name for your feelings.*

HEARTWORK EXERCISE 2: THE EMOTIONS

TIP: *Once you've identified a situation that didn't turn out as you had hoped, take a deep breath. Afterward, describe the situation and note who else (if anyone) was involved. Then, write down how the situation made you feel. What thoughts and emotions arise as you revisit the memory? How did it make you feel? Use the emotion wheel to find the most appropriate name for your feelings.*

GIVE THE SITUATION A NAME

WHO WAS INVOLVED?

WHAT HAPPENED?

FEELINGS

PARENT FEELINGS

HEARTWORK EXERCISE 2: THE EMOTIONS

TIP: *Once you've identified a situation that didn't turn out as you had hoped, take a deep breath. Afterward, describe the situation and note who else (if anyone) was involved. Then, write down how the situation made you feel. What thoughts and emotions arise as you revisit the memory? How did it make you feel? Use the emotion wheel to find the most appropriate name for your feelings.*

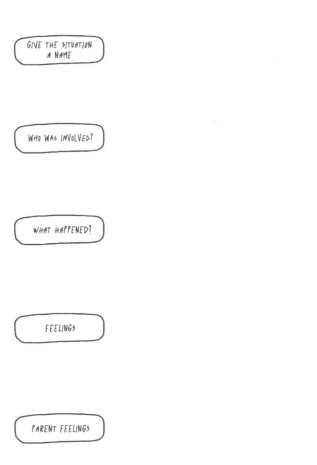

HEARTWORK EXERCISE 2: THE EMOTIONS

TIP: *Once you've identified a situation that didn't turn out as you had hoped, take a deep breath. Afterward, describe the situation and note who else (if anyone) was involved. Then, write down how the situation made you feel. What thoughts and emotions arise as you revisit the memory? How did it make you feel? Use the emotion wheel to find the most appropriate name for your feelings.*

GIVE THE SITUATION
A NAME

WHO WAS INVOLVED?

WHAT HAPPENED?

FEELINGS

PARENT FEELINGS

HEART
~~HOME~~WORK EXERCISE 3

HEARTWORK EXERCISE 3: THE PATTERN

Now that you've mapped out the events, your feelings about them, and the *parent* feelings, the next step is to trace the emotional patterns that emerge when you experience similar events. To do that, use the chart below.

Diving into Heartwork Exercise Two, we're going to get really clear on what's been happening in those key moments of your life. The goal is to spot patterns by breaking down each event into three simple parts: the facts (what happened), your feelings about it (how it made you feel in the moment), and the parent feelings (the broader emotions those feelings tap into). Just stick to what's common across the experiences you've listed—facts, feelings, and parent feelings.

Let's go:

Analyze and list the facts, feelings, and overarching parent feelings from each significant event listed in Heartwork Exercise Two. Only list the facts, feelings and parent feelings that are present in every event you wrote down.

From there, do the same with your feelings. Only list feelings appeared consistently when similar events or circumstances occurred.

TIP: Pay special attention to any emotion that comes up repeatedly when you experience different but similar events. This methodical approach will help you visually connect the dots between recurring feelings and the situations that evoke them to give you a clearer understanding of the emotional patterns at play in your life.

HEARTWORK EXERCISE 3: THE PATTERN

TIP: *Pay special attention to any emotion that comes up repeatedly when you experience different but similar events. This methodical approach will help you visually connect the dots between recurring feelings and the situations that evoke them to give you a clearer understanding of the emotional patterns at play in your life.*

WHICH FACTS ARE
PRESENT IN EACH
EVENT?

WHICH FEELINGS ARE
PRESENT IN EACH
EVENT?

WHICH PARENT FEELINGS
ARE PRESENT IN EACH
EVENT?

HEARTWORK EXERCISE 3: THE PATTERN

TIP: *Pay special attention to any emotion that comes up repeatedly when you experience different but similar events. This methodical approach will help you visually connect the dots between recurring feelings and the situations that evoke them to give you a clearer understanding of the emotional patterns at play in your life.*

WHICH FACTS ARE
PRESENT IN EACH
EVENT?

WHICH FEELINGS ARE
PRESENT IN EACH
EVENT?

WHICH PARENT FEELINGS
ARE PRESENT IN EACH
EVENT?

HEARTWORK EXERCISE 3: THE PATTERN

TIP: *Pay special attention to any emotion that comes up repeatedly when you experience different but similar events. This methodical approach will help you visually connect the dots between recurring feelings and the situations that evoke them to give you a clearer understanding of the emotional patterns at play in your life.*

WHICH FACTS ARE
PRESENT IN EACH
EVENT?

WHICH FEELINGS ARE
PRESENT IN EACH
EVENT?

WHICH PARENT FEELINGS
ARE PRESENT IN EACH
EVENT?

HEARTWORK EXERCISE 3: THE PATTERN

TIP: *Pay special attention to any emotion that comes up repeatedly when you experience different but similar events. This methodical approach will help you visually connect the dots between recurring feelings and the situations that evoke them to give you a clearer understanding of the emotional patterns at play in your life.*

WHICH FACTS ARE
PRESENT IN EACH
EVENT?

WHICH FEELINGS ARE
PRESENT IN EACH
EVENT?

WHICH PARENT FEELINGS
ARE PRESENT IN EACH
EVENT?

HEARTWORK EXERCISE 3: THE PATTERN

TIP: *Pay special attention to any emotion that comes up repeatedly when you experience different but similar events. This methodical approach will help you visually connect the dots between recurring feelings and the situations that evoke them to give you a clearer understanding of the emotional patterns at play in your life.*

WHICH FACTS ARE
PRESENT IN EACH
EVENT?

WHICH FEELINGS ARE
PRESENT IN EACH
EVENT?

WHICH PARENT FEELINGS
ARE PRESENT IN EACH
EVENT?

HEARTWORK EXERCISE 3: THE PATTERN

TIP: Pay special attention to any emotion that comes up repeatedly when you experience different but similar events. This methodical approach will help you visually connect the dots between recurring feelings and the situations that evoke them to give you a clearer understanding of the emotional patterns at play in your life.

WHICH FACTS ARE
PRESENT IN EACH
EVENT?

WHICH FEELINGS ARE
PRESENT IN EACH
EVENT?

WHICH PARENT FEELINGS
ARE PRESENT IN EACH
EVENT?

HEARTWORK EXERCISE 3: THE PATTERN

TIP: *Pay special attention to any emotion that comes up repeatedly when you experience different but similar events. This methodical approach will help you visually connect the dots between recurring feelings and the situations that evoke them to give you a clearer understanding of the emotional patterns at play in your life.*

WHICH FACTS ARE
PRESENT IN EACH
EVENT?

WHICH FEELINGS ARE
PRESENT IN EACH
EVENT?

WHICH PARENT FEELINGS
ARE PRESENT IN EACH
EVENT?

HEARTWORK EXERCISE 3: THE PATTERN

TIP: *Pay special attention to any emotion that comes up repeatedly when you experience different but similar events. This methodical approach will help you visually connect the dots between recurring feelings and the situations that evoke them to give you a clearer understanding of the emotional patterns at play in your life.*

WHICH FACTS ARE
PRESENT IN EACH
EVENT?

WHICH FEELINGS ARE
PRESENT IN EACH
EVENT?

WHICH PARENT FEELINGS
ARE PRESENT IN EACH
EVENT?

HEARTWORK EXERCISE 3: THE PATTERN

TIP: *Pay special attention to any emotion that comes up repeatedly when you experience different but similar events. This methodical approach will help you visually connect the dots between recurring feelings and the situations that evoke them to give you a clearer understanding of the emotional patterns at play in your life.*

WHICH FACTS ARE PRESENT IN EACH EVENT?

WHICH FEELINGS ARE PRESENT IN EACH EVENT?

WHICH PARENT FEELINGS ARE PRESENT IN EACH EVENT?

HEARTWORK EXERCISE 3: THE PATTERN

TIP: *Pay special attention to any emotion that comes up repeatedly when you experience different but similar events. This methodical approach will help you visually connect the dots between recurring feelings and the situations that evoke them to give you a clearer understanding of the emotional patterns at play in your life.*

WHICH FACTS ARE
PRESENT IN EACH
EVENT?

WHICH FEELINGS ARE
PRESENT IN EACH
EVENT?

WHICH PARENT FEELINGS
ARE PRESENT IN EACH
EVENT?

HEARTWORK EXERCISE 3: THE PATTERN

TIP: *Pay special attention to any emotion that comes up repeatedly when you experience different but similar events. This methodical approach will help you visually connect the dots between recurring feelings and the situations that evoke them to give you a clearer understanding of the emotional patterns at play in your life.*

WHICH FACTS ARE
PRESENT IN EACH
EVENT?

WHICH FEELINGS ARE
PRESENT IN EACH
EVENT?

WHICH PARENT FEELINGS
ARE PRESENT IN EACH
EVENT?

HEART ~~HOME~~WORK EXERCISE 4

HEARTWORK EXERCISE 4: THE FIRST EVENT

Understanding the 'firsts' often clarifies the 'nows.' So please take a step back and look at how you got here.

You've been doing some serious detective work on yourself. You've identified similarities in events and pinpointed the feelings that come with them.

Now, you're about to dive into something fascinating. You're going to figure out where those feelings started. It's like going on a treasure hunt into your past, seeking that "aha" moment when those feelings first popped up.

This exercise requires you to be kind and patient with yourself as you sift through your memories. Please remember, you are not here to beat yourself up over what you find or wish things were different. Instead, you should aim to understand where and when those feelings and situations first took root in your emotional framework.

Think about the events and emotions you uncovered in the previous exercises.

Reflect on the very first time you encountered those specific facts and feelings in your life. What went down? Your aim is to identify the initial instance when an event—akin to those you noted in Heartwork Exercises Two and Three—triggered these emotions for you.

Please remember to take your time. Find a safe, private space. Sit comfortably and quietly with one hand on your heart and the other on your stomach. Take a deep breath. Now go inward, and perhaps you can remember the first time you had that feeling and the event associated with it.

When you remember, fill in the blank below.

TIP: *Take your time with this. It's about connecting the dots. Go as far back in your memory as you can. You're on the lookout for the first time an event brought about similar feelings to the one(s) listed in Heartwork Exercises Two and Three.*

A. The first time I ever had this feeling was when

_____

HEARTWORK EXERCISE 4: THE FIRST EVENT

TIP: *Take your time with this. It's about connecting the dots. Go as far back in your memory as you can. You're on the lookout for the first time an event brought about similar feelings to the one(s) listed in Heartwork Exercises Two and Three.*

A. The first time I ever had this feeling was when
_____.

HEARTWORK EXERCISE 4: THE FIRST EVENT

TIP: *Take your time with this. It's about connecting the dots. Go as far back in your memory as you can. You're on the lookout for the first time an event brought about similar feelings to the one(s) listed in Heartwork Exercises Two and Three.*

   A. The first time I ever had this feeling was when
   _____.

HEARTWORK EXERCISE 4: THE FIRST EVENT

TIP: *Take your time with this. It's about connecting the dots. Go as far back in your memory as you can. You're on the lookout for the first time an event brought about similar feelings to the one(s) listed in Heartwork Exercises Two and Three.*

    A. The first time I ever had this feeling was when

_____

HEARTWORK EXERCISE 4: THE FIRST EVENT

TIP: *Take your time with this. It's about connecting the dots. Go as far back in your memory as you can. You're on the lookout for the first time an event brought about similar feelings to the one(s) listed in Heartwork Exercises Two and Three.*

    A. The first time I ever had this feeling was when _____

HEARTWORK EXERCISE 4: THE FIRST EVENT

TIP: *Take your time with this. It's about connecting the dots. Go as far back in your memory as you can. You're on the lookout for the first time an event brought about similar feelings to the one(s) listed in Heartwork Exercises Two and Three.*

A. The first time I ever had this feeling was when
_____.

HEARTWORK EXERCISE 4: THE FIRST EVENT

TIP: *Take your time with this. It's about connecting the dots. Go as far back in your memory as you can. You're on the lookout for the first time an event brought about similar feelings to the one(s) listed in Heartwork Exercises Two and Three.*

A. The first time I ever had this feeling was when
_____.

HEARTWORK EXERCISE 4: THE FIRST EVENT

TIP: *Take your time with this. It's about connecting the dots. Go as far back in your memory as you can. You're on the lookout for the first time an event brought about similar feelings to the one(s) listed in Heartwork Exercises Two and Three.*

A. **The first time I ever had this feeling was when**
_____

HEARTWORK EXERCISE 4: THE FIRST EVENT

TIP: *Take your time with this. It's about connecting the dots. Go as far back in your memory as you can. You're on the lookout for the first time an event brought about similar feelings to the one(s) listed in Heartwork Exercises Two and Three.*

    A. The first time I ever had this feeling was when

    _____

HEARTWORK EXERCISE 4: THE FIRST EVENT

TIP: *Take your time with this. It's about connecting the dots. Go as far back in your memory as you can. You're on the lookout for the first time an event brought about similar feelings to the one(s) listed in Heartwork Exercises Two and Three.*

A. The first time I ever had this feeling was when

_____

HEARTWORK EXERCISE 4: THE FIRST EVENT

TIP: *Take your time with this. It's about connecting the dots. Go as far back in your memory as you can. You're on the lookout for the first time an event brought about similar feelings to the one(s) listed in Heartwork Exercises Two and Three.*

A. The first time I ever had this feeling was when
_____.

CHAPTER 5

GERMINATION:

CRACKING OPEN YOUR FEELINGS TO FIND WHAT'S INSIDE

Think of germination, when a seed finally cracks open after hanging out in the perfect mix of warmth and water. It's the start of something new, something alive. This chapter, Germination, is like that for you. It's about breaking open in a way that will let you discover what you needed then and what you need when you experience the same (or similar) emotion again.

This chapter's heartwork exercises will help you see your emotions as messengers. Each exercise will give you a clue about your deepest unmet needs, the things you've longed for. The heartwork will help you to recognize your unmet needs and figure out how to give yourself the love and care you've been missing.

To prepare you for your heartwork, let's explore emotions (Parent Feelings): fear, anger, sadness, joy, surprise, and love. These are fundamental human emotions that have various primal purposes.

Fear is a primal emotion. It triggers the fight, flight or freeze response to a perceived threat. It's a protective mechanism to deal with perceived danger.

Anger arises in response to the perception of being wronged or harmed. It can be a catalyst for addressing injustice or setting boundaries.

Sadness is a reflective emotion that often arises from experiences of loss or disappointment. It can lead to introspection and sometimes provide the necessary space to process and heal from those experiences.

Joy is an emotion of great pleasure and happiness. It often arises from experiences of success, fulfillment, or connection with others. It can reinforce behaviors that lead to positive outcomes.

Surprise is a brief emotional state that comes from experiencing something unexpected. It can be positive, negative, or neutral and helps us focus on new information.

Love is a complex set of emotions and attitudes associated with intense affection, protectiveness, warmth, and respect for others. It can also apply to objects, principles, and oneself. It frequently underlies deep interpersonal bonds.

Each of the emotions above plays a crucial role in our lives. They influence our behavior, decision-making, and relationships with others. The more challenging ones, like fear, anger, and sadness, are often clues to what you've been missing–and that's what this chapter explores.

Think of these emotions as signs pointing toward needs you didn't even know you had. Perhaps your fear is because you crave safety, or your anger is because you need to be respected. And your sadness? That might be because you need to feel connected to others.

No matter what it is, diving into your feelings lets you piece together the puzzle of your unmet needs. It will help you understand what you were reaching for in those moments that shaped your identity.

HEART

~~HOME~~WORK EXERCISE 5

HEARTWORK EXERCISE 5: UNMET NEED

This heartwork exercise aims to deepen your understanding of how specific *parent* feelings, the ones identified in the emotion wheel, link to unmet needs. By examining the emotions you identified in Heartwork Exercise Three, you will see patterns that connect those feelings to underlying needs that were not met the first time you felt them.

Remembering and being familiar with the event that provoked the first time you felt an intense emotion is pivotal in your emotional growth. Why? Because that is probably when you first established an unhealthy or undesirable behavior pattern. That was the moment when you adapted in the best way you knew how. It's essential to be kind to yourself about how you responded; those were the only tools you had at your disposal at the time. That was the only way you had to get your needs met. Those events and the emotions that followed have become learned behavior.

Having your needs met is fundamental to your well-being. You thrive when your needs, safety, love, respect, or connection are fulfilled. When they're not met, you find ways, consciously or unconsciously, to cope.

Recognizing those early feelings from that very first event will help you to understand your need that went unmet. It is crucial that you know that because it points you directly to the root of your patterns. By identifying your initial unmet need, you can see why you've repeated certain behaviors or found yourself in subsequent similar situations.

You will always, consciously or unconsciously, do what you know how to do to meet your needs. We all do. Even if the avenue we take to get that need met is unhealthy or doesn't work well for you now, it served you then. However, you have better ways to get your needs met now, even if you don't know what that better way is yet.

Please remember, in your younger years, you developed specific behaviors as your best attempt to meet your needs. But, those behaviors created patterns that don't deliver the fulfillment you seek now. In fact, they often do the exact opposite. They inadvertently lead you to the very outcomes you wish to avoid.

It's like uncovering an old map you drew as a kid, only to realize you've been following paths that don't take you where you want to go anymore.

The following heartwork exercise will help you connect the dots between the feelings and behaviors you have now and the needs you tried to meet way back when.

By spotting where those patterns began, you can find new routes that genuinely lead to the safety, love, respect, and connection you crave.

Step 1: Review Your Previous Work

Begin by revisiting Heartwork Exercise Three, where you listed your *parent* feelings: The broader emotional states like fear, anger, and sadness that are umbrellas for more specific feelings you've experienced. The recurring facts, feelings and parent feelings listed in Heartwork Exercise 3 is what will point you to your unmet need.

Step 2: Connect Emotions to Needs

Use the list below to match your *parent* feelings and unmet needs. The list isn't exhaustive but is a starting point to explore the needs often associated with the respective feelings. This exercise is not about finding a one-size-fits-all answer but exploring your emotional landscape to understand what you've been seeking at various times. If a specific unmet need doesn't immediately stand out, that's okay. This process is about exploration and reflection. Allow yourself the space and grace to uncover one layer at a time.

Please remember that these emotional responses to unmet needs are not exhaustive or exclusive. Some people experience a complex blend of emotions in response to a single unmet need. Similarly, a single emotion can be linked to multiple unmet needs.

As you go through them, use your dominant feeling as a guide. Ask yourself:

"Based on the parent feelings(s) I've identified in Heartwork Exercise Three, what need went unmet?"

Use the *parent* feelings as a guide.

Fear is often linked to unmet needs for:

☐ Safety: The need to feel secure in your environment.

☐ Certainty: The need to have predictability and stability in your life.

☐ Autonomy: The need to feel in control of your life and decisions.

Anger might be experienced when there are unmet needs for:

- ❐ Respect: The need to be treated with consideration and understanding.

- ❐ Fairness: The need to be treated justly and receive equitable treatment.

- ❐ Boundary Integrity: The need to have your boundaries acknowledged and maintained.

Sadness can be a response to unmet needs such as:

- ❐ Connection: The need to have a sense of belonging or companionship.

- ❐ Love: The need to give and receive affection.

- ❐ Achievement: The need to reach your goals and fulfill your potential.

Step 3 Identifying Your Unmet Need

In your journal, next to each of the *parent* feelings, circle the unmet need that most resonates with your experience.

Step 4 Fill Out The Reflection Prompt

Fill out the following prompt and insert your corresponding unmet need.

Common Unmet Needs and Their *Parent* Feelings

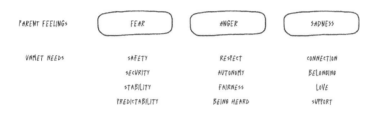

PARENT FEELINGS — FEAR — ANGER — SADNESS

UNMET NEEDS

FEAR	ANGER	SADNESS
SAFETY	RESPECT	CONNECTION
SECURITY	AUTONOMY	BELONGING
STABILITY	FAIRNESS	LOVE
PREDICTABILITY	BEING HEARD	SUPPORT

B. **"When I revisit the event that first sparked this feeling(s), I recognize I was actually seeking _____, which, at the time, went unfulfilled."** (*unmet need*)

TIP: *The connection between emotions and unmet needs is deeply personal. If a particular need doesn't stand out immediately, give yourself permission to explore and reflect. This exercise isn't about pinpointing a definitive answer but understanding your emotional landscape and the desires that have shaped your journey.*

HEARTWORK EXERCISE 5: UNMET NEED

TIP: *The connection between emotions and unmet needs is deeply personal. If a particular need doesn't stand out immediately, give yourself permission to explore and reflect. This exercise isn't about pinpointing a definitive answer but understanding your emotional landscape and the desires that have shaped your journey.*

Common Unmet Needs and Their *Parent* Feelings

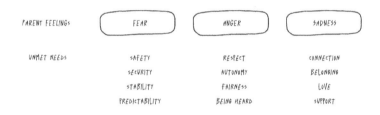

PARENT FEELINGS   FEAR   ANGER   SADNESS

UNMET NEEDS		
SAFETY	RESPECT	CONNECTION
SECURITY	AUTONOMY	BELONGING
STABILITY	FAIRNESS	LOVE
PREDICTABILITY	BEING HEARD	SUPPORT

B "When I revisit the event that first sparked this feeling(s), I recognize I was actually seeking _____, which, at the time, went unfulfilled."   *(unmet need)*

HEARTWORK EXERCISE 5: UNMET NEED

TIP: The connection between emotions and unmet needs is deeply personal. If a particular need doesn't stand out immediately, give yourself permission to explore and reflect. This exercise isn't about pinpointing a definitive answer but understanding your emotional landscape and the desires that have shaped your journey.

Common Unmet Needs and Their *Parent* Feelings

PARENT FEELINGS   FEAR   ANGER   SADNESS

UNMET NEEDS	SAFETY	RESPECT	CONNECTION
	SECURITY	AUTONOMY	BELONGING
	STABILITY	FAIRNESS	LOVE
	PREDICTABILITY	BEING HEARD	SUPPORT

B   "When I revisit the event that first sparked this feeling(s), I recognize I was actually seeking _____, which, at the time, went unfulfilled."   *(unmet need)*

HEARTWORK EXERCISE 5: UNMET NEED

TIP: *The connection between emotions and unmet needs is deeply personal. If a particular need doesn't stand out immediately, give yourself permission to explore and reflect. This exercise isn't about pinpointing a definitive answer but understanding your emotional landscape and the desires that have shaped your journey.*

Common Unmet Needs and Their *Parent* Feelings

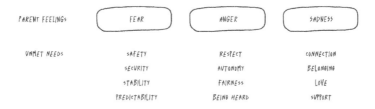

PARENT FEELINGS	FEAR	ANGER	SADNESS
UNMET NEEDS	SAFETY	RESPECT	CONNECTION
	SECURITY	AUTONOMY	BELONGING
	STABILITY	FAIRNESS	LOVE
	PREDICTABILITY	BEING HEARD	SUPPORT

B **"When I revisit the event that first sparked this feeling(s), I recognize I was actually seeking _____, which, at the time, went unfulfilled."** *(unmet need)*

HEARTWORK EXERCISE 5: UNMET NEED

TIP: *The connection between emotions and unmet needs is deeply personal. If a particular need doesn't stand out immediately, give yourself permission to explore and reflect. This exercise isn't about pinpointing a definitive answer but understanding your emotional landscape and the desires that have shaped your journey.*

Common Unmet Needs and Their *Parent* Feelings

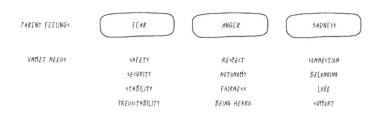

B   "When   I   revisit   the   event   that   first   sparked this   feeling(s),   I   recognize   I   was   actually   seeking _____, which, at the time, went unfulfilled."   *(unmet need)*

HEARTWORK EXERCISE 5: UNMET NEED

TIP: *The connection between emotions and unmet needs is deeply personal. If a particular need doesn't stand out immediately, give yourself permission to explore and reflect. This exercise isn't about pinpointing a definitive answer but understanding your emotional landscape and the desires that have shaped your journey.*

Common Unmet Needs and Their *Parent* Feelings

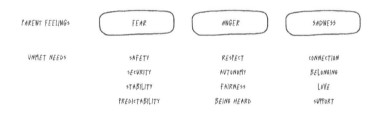

PARENT FEELINGS	FEAR	ANGER	SADNESS
UNMET NEEDS	SAFETY	RESPECT	CONNECTION
	SECURITY	AUTONOMY	BELONGING
	STABILITY	FAIRNESS	LOVE
	PREDICTABILITY	BEING HEARD	SUPPORT

B   "When I revisit the event that first sparked this feeling(s), I recognize I was actually seeking _____, which, at the time, went unfulfilled."   (*unmet need*)

HEARTWORK EXERCISE 5: UNMET NEED

TIP: *The connection between emotions and unmet needs is deeply personal. If a particular need doesn't stand out immediately, give yourself permission to explore and reflect. This exercise isn't about pinpointing a definitive answer but understanding your emotional landscape and the desires that have shaped your journey.*

Common Unmet Needs and Their *Parent* Feelings

PARENT FEELINGS	FEAR	ANGER	SADNESS
UNMET NEEDS	SAFETY	RESPECT	CONNECTION
	SECURITY	AUTONOMY	BELONGING
	STABILITY	FAIRNESS	LOVE
	PREDICTABILITY	BEING HEARD	SUPPORT

B   "When I revisit the event that first sparked this feeling(s), I recognize I was actually seeking _____, which, at the time, went unfulfilled."   *(unmet need)*

HEARTWORK EXERCISE 5: UNMET NEED

TIP: The connection between emotions and unmet needs is deeply personal. If a particular need doesn't stand out immediately, give yourself permission to explore and reflect. This exercise isn't about pinpointing a definitive answer but understanding your emotional landscape and the desires that have shaped your journey.

Common Unmet Needs and Their *Parent* Feelings

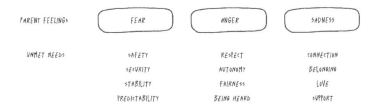

PARENT FEELINGS	FEAR	ANGER	SADNESS
UNMET NEEDS	SAFETY	RESPECT	CONNECTION
	SECURITY	AUTONOMY	BELONGING
	STABILITY	FAIRNESS	LOVE
	PREDICTABILITY	BEING HEARD	SUPPORT

B   "When I revisit the event that first sparked this feeling(s), I recognize I was actually seeking _____, which, at the time, went unfulfilled."   (*unmet need*)

HEARTWORK EXERCISE 5: UNMET NEED

TIP: *The connection between emotions and unmet needs is deeply personal. If a particular need doesn't stand out immediately, give yourself permission to explore and reflect. This exercise isn't about pinpointing a definitive answer but understanding your emotional landscape and the desires that have shaped your journey.*

Common Unmet Needs and Their *Parent* Feelings

PARENT FEELINGS   FEAR   ANGER   SADNESS

UNMET NEEDS	SAFETY	RESPECT	CONNECTION
	SECURITY	AUTONOMY	BELONGING
	STABILITY	FAIRNESS	LOVE
	PREDICTABILITY	BEING HEARD	SUPPORT

B   "When I revisit the event that first sparked this feeling(s), I recognize I was actually seeking _____, which, at the time, went unfulfilled."   *(unmet need)*

HEARTWORK EXERCISE 5: UNMET NEED

TIP: The connection between emotions and unmet needs is deeply personal. If a particular need doesn't stand out immediately, give yourself permission to explore and reflect. This exercise isn't about pinpointing a definitive answer but understanding your emotional landscape and the desires that have shaped your journey.

Common Unmet Needs and Their *Parent* Feelings

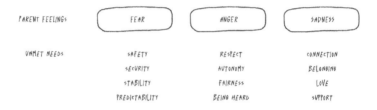

PARENT FEELINGS	FEAR	ANGER	SADNESS
UNMET NEEDS	SAFETY	RESPECT	CONNECTION
	SECURITY	AUTONOMY	BELONGING
	STABILITY	FAIRNESS	LOVE
	PREDICTABILITY	BEING HEARD	SUPPORT

B   "When I revisit the event that first sparked this feeling(s), I recognize I was actually seeking _____, which, at the time, went unfulfilled."   *(unmet need)*

HEARTWORK EXERCISE 5: UNMET NEED

TIP: *The connection between emotions and unmet needs is deeply personal. If a particular need doesn't stand out immediately, give yourself permission to explore and reflect. This exercise isn't about pinpointing a definitive answer but understanding your emotional landscape and the desires that have shaped your journey.*

Common Unmet Needs and Their *Parent* Feelings

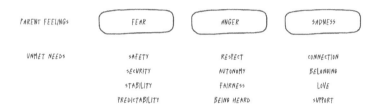

B   "When   I   revisit   the   event   that   first   sparked this   feeling(s),   I   recognize   I   was   actually   seeking _____, which, at the time, went unfulfilled."   *(unmet need)*

HEARTWORK EXERCISE 5: UNMET NEED

TIP: *The connection between emotions and unmet needs is deeply personal. If a particular need doesn't stand out immediately, give yourself permission to explore and reflect. This exercise isn't about pinpointing a definitive answer but understanding your emotional landscape and the desires that have shaped your journey.*

Common Unmet Needs and Their *Parent* Feelings

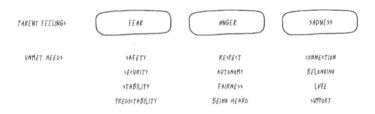

PARENT FEELINGS	FEAR	ANGER	SADNESS
UNMET NEEDS	SAFETY	RESPECT	CONNECTION
	SECURITY	AUTONOMY	BELONGING
	STABILITY	FAIRNESS	LOVE
	PREDICTABILITY	BEING HEARD	SUPPORT

B   "When I revisit the event that first sparked this feeling(s), I recognize I was actually seeking _____, which, at the time, went unfulfilled."   (*unmet need*)

CHAPTER 6

DISCOVERING YOUR COPING MECHANISMS

O n life's rollercoaster ride, coping mechanisms are your safety harnesses. They're the strategies and behaviors you develop to manage the emotional ups and downs, especially when stressed or uncomfortable. But how did you come up with your coping mechanisms? The answer is simple yet complex. As you faced challenges, your mind and body naturally sought ways to protect yourself, ease the pain, or confront the situation head-on. These mechanisms were born out of necessity, tailored by your experiences, beliefs, and the environment you found yourself in.

Coping mechanisms often show up when needs are unmet. Think of them as your psyche attempting to fill a void or regain control when you feel vulnerable. Whether seeking a connection to combat loneliness or engaging in physical activity to dissipate anger, these strategies are your personal toolkit for emotional survival. Yet, understanding when and how these coping mechanisms manifest depends on your awareness. Some may serve you well, offering solace and strength, while others might lead to more challenges, underscoring the importance of discerning their impact on your life.

To truly comprehend our coping mechanisms, we must delve into the fear that underlies them. This fear is what we're ultimately trying to shield ourselves from with our coping strategies. Recognizing this fear is crucial as it directs us to the specific coping mechanisms we employ to feel safe. By identifying the fear, we can then unravel the nature of our coping strategies—whether they are constructive or detrimental to our growth.

The following heartwork exercise invites you to delve into the origins of your coping mechanisms. Through this introspection, you'll better understand your resilience and how you've instinctively learned to care for yourself amid adversity. This exercise isn't just about identifying your coping mechanism(s); it's about recognizing their value, understanding their roots, and considering how they might limit or empower you. But be patient; soon, you will also explore how they serve you in positive ways. As you move forward, approach this exploration with openness and curiosity to honor the wisdom in your coping strategies, and allow this understanding to illuminate the path to managing your fears more effectively.

HAPPINESS
DOESN'T
COME FROM
HOLDING ON.

BUTTERFLY SZN

HEART

~~HOME~~WORK EXERCISE 6

HEARTWORK EXERCISE 6: FEAR

Before you dive into the next exercise, please take a moment to understand the foundation of what you're about to explore.

This exercise focuses on uncovering what you've been trying to protect yourself from. At the heart of your protection often lies fear: fear of being hurt, fear of rejection, or any number of deep-seated anxieties that you might not always be ready to face directly.

Fear is a powerful force. It often drives us to adopt specific coping mechanisms, especially when we find ourselves in circumstances reminiscent of past pains or challenges. These mechanisms are our mind's way of shielding us from similar discomforts. However, by continually relying on the same protective strategies, we might find ourselves stuck in a loop, repeating patterns without genuinely addressing the root cause of our fears.

Heartwork Exercise Six is a culmination, where identifying your emotions, understanding your unmet needs, as well as understanding your fear comes together.

So, delve into this exercise with a gentle spirit and an open heart. Remember, there's no rush and no right or wrong answers. You may uncover a single fear or a complex web of anxieties and wounds. Whatever you discover, know it's a valid and significant step on your journey. Embrace this opportunity to shine a light on your fears because understanding them is the first step toward overcoming them and finding healthier ways to cope in the future.

Fill in the blank, 'When I revisit the event, I realized in that situation, I needed (*unmet need*) , but that need went unmet.

C. This sparked the fear of _____
_____.

(*what were you afraid of happening? What did worse case scenario look like?*)

Understanding the fear behind what you've been protecting yourself from is crucial to breaking free from repetitive cycles and moving forward on your path of healing, self-discovery, and empowerment.

TIP: *As you fill in the blank, think about the actions or behaviors you tend to default to when faced with the fears you've identified above. Whether withdrawing from others, overworking, seeking constant reassurance, or any other strategy, this is about recognizing how you've tried to shield yourself. Reflect on how your coping mechanisms have served you in the past and consider their effectiveness in genuinely addressing the underlying fear. This introspection is crucial to acknowledging the patterns you've created to respond to fear. They set the stage for exploring new, healthier ways to deal with your feelings.*

HEARTWORK EXERCISE 6: FEAR

TIP: As you fill in the blank, think about the actions or behaviors you tend to default to when faced with the fears you've identified above. Whether withdrawing from others, overworking, seeking constant reassurance, or any other strategy, this is about recognizing how you've tried to shield yourself. Reflect on how your coping mechanisms have served you in the past and consider their effectiveness in genuinely addressing the underlying fear. This introspection is crucial to acknowledging the patterns you've created to respond to fear. They set the stage for exploring new, healthier ways to deal with your feelings.

Fill in the blank, 'When I revisit the event, I realized in that situation, I needed _____ **, but that need went unmet.** *(unmet need)*

C. This sparked the fear of _____
. *(what were you afraid of happening? What did worse case scenario look like?)*

Understanding the fear behind what you've been protecting yourself from is crucial to breaking free from repetitive cycles and moving forward on your path of healing, self-discovery, and empowerment.

HEARTWORK EXERCISE 6: FEAR

TIP: *As you fill in the blank, think about the actions or behaviors you tend to default to when faced with the fears you've identified above. Whether withdrawing from others, overworking, seeking constant reassurance, or any other strategy, this is about recognizing how you've tried to shield yourself. Reflect on how your coping mechanisms have served you in the past and consider their effectiveness in genuinely addressing the underlying fear. This introspection is crucial to acknowledging the patterns you've created to respond to fear. They set the stage for exploring new, healthier ways to deal with your feelings.*

Fill in the blank, 'When I revisit the event, I realized in that situation, I needed _____ , but that need went unmet. (*unmet need*)

C. This sparked the fear of _____
. (*what were you afraid of happening? What did worse case scenario look like?*)

Understanding the fear behind what you've been protecting yourself from is crucial to breaking free from repetitive cycles and moving forward on your path of healing, self-discovery, and empowerment.

HEARTWORK EXERCISE 6: FEAR

TIP: *As you fill in the blank, think about the actions or behaviors you tend to default to when faced with the fears you've identified above. Whether withdrawing from others, overworking, seeking constant reassurance, or any other strategy, this is about recognizing how you've tried to shield yourself. Reflect on how your coping mechanisms have served you in the past and consider their effectiveness in genuinely addressing the underlying fear. This introspection is crucial to acknowledging the patterns you've created to respond to fear. They set the stage for exploring new, healthier ways to deal with your feelings.*

Fill in the blank, 'When I revisit the event, I realized in that situation, I needed _____ **, but that need went unmet.** *(unmet need)*

C. This sparked the fear of _____
. *(what were you afraid of happening? What did worse case scenario look like?)*

Understanding the fear behind what you've been protecting yourself from is crucial to breaking free from repetitive cycles and moving forward on your path of healing, self-discovery, and empowerment.

HEARTWORK EXERCISE 6: FEAR

TIP: *As you fill in the blank, think about the actions or behaviors you tend to default to when faced with the fears you've identified above. Whether withdrawing from others, overworking, seeking constant reassurance, or any other strategy, this is about recognizing how you've tried to shield yourself. Reflect on how your coping mechanisms have served you in the past and consider their effectiveness in genuinely addressing the underlying fear. This introspection is crucial to acknowledging the patterns you've created to respond to fear. They set the stage for exploring new, healthier ways to deal with your feelings.*

Fill in the blank, 'When I revisit the event, I realized in that situation, I needed ———————————————————— **, but that need went unmet.** (*unmet need*)

C. This sparked the fear of ————————————————
. (*what were you afraid of happening? What did worse case scenario look like?*)

Understanding the fear behind what you've been protecting yourself from is crucial to breaking free from repetitive cycles and moving forward on your path of healing, self-discovery, and empowerment.

HEARTWORK EXERCISE 6: FEAR

TIP: *As you fill in the blank, think about the actions or behaviors you tend to default to when faced with the fears you've identified above. Whether withdrawing from others, overworking, seeking constant reassurance, or any other strategy, this is about recognizing how you've tried to shield yourself. Reflect on how your coping mechanisms have served you in the past and consider their effectiveness in genuinely addressing the underlying fear. This introspection is crucial to acknowledging the patterns you've created to respond to fear. They set the stage for exploring new, healthier ways to deal with your feelings.*

Fill in the blank, 'When I revisit the event, I realized in that situation, I needed _____ , but that need went unmet. *(unmet need)*

C. This sparked the fear of _____

. (*what were you afraid of happening? What did worse case scenario look like?*)

Understanding the fear behind what you've been protecting yourself from is crucial to breaking free from repetitive cycles and moving forward on your path of healing, self-discovery, and empowerment.

HEARTWORK EXERCISE 6: FEAR

TIP: *As you fill in the blank, think about the actions or behaviors you tend to default to when faced with the fears you've identified above. Whether withdrawing from others, overworking, seeking constant reassurance, or any other strategy, this is about recognizing how you've tried to shield yourself. Reflect on how your coping mechanisms have served you in the past and consider their effectiveness in genuinely addressing the underlying fear. This introspection is crucial to acknowledging the patterns you've created to respond to fear. They set the stage for exploring new, healthier ways to deal with your feelings.*

Fill in the blank, 'When I revisit the event, I realized in that situation, I needed _____ , but that need went unmet. *(unmet need)*

C. This sparked the fear of _____
. *(what were you afraid of happening? What did worse case scenario look like?)*

Understanding the fear behind what you've been protecting yourself from is crucial to breaking free from repetitive cycles and moving forward on your path of healing, self-discovery, and empowerment.

HEARTWORK EXERCISE 6: FEAR

TIP: *As you fill in the blank, think about the actions or behaviors you tend to default to when faced with the fears you've identified above. Whether withdrawing from others, overworking, seeking constant reassurance, or any other strategy, this is about recognizing how you've tried to shield yourself. Reflect on how your coping mechanisms have served you in the past and consider their effectiveness in genuinely addressing the underlying fear. This introspection is crucial to acknowledging the patterns you've created to respond to fear. They set the stage for exploring new, healthier ways to deal with your feelings.*

Fill in the blank, 'When I revisit the event, I realized in that situation, I needed _____ , but that need went unmet. *(unmet need)*

C. This sparked the fear of _____
. (*what were you afraid of happening? What did worse case scenario look like?*)

Understanding the fear behind what you've been protecting yourself from is crucial to breaking free from repetitive cycles and moving forward on your path of healing, self-discovery, and empowerment.

HEARTWORK EXERCISE 6: FEAR

TIP: As you fill in the blank, think about the actions or behaviors you tend to default to when faced with the fears you've identified above. Whether withdrawing from others, overworking, seeking constant reassurance, or any other strategy, this is about recognizing how you've tried to shield yourself. Reflect on how your coping mechanisms have served you in the past and consider their effectiveness in genuinely addressing the underlying fear. This introspection is crucial to acknowledging the patterns you've created to respond to fear. They set the stage for exploring new, healthier ways to deal with your feelings.

Fill in the blank, 'When I revisit the event, I realized in that situation, I needed _____ , but that need went unmet.   *(unmet need)*

C. This sparked the fear of _____
. *(what were you afraid of happening? What did worse case scenario look like?)*

Understanding the fear behind what you've been protecting yourself from is crucial to breaking free from repetitive cycles and moving forward on your path of healing, self-discovery, and empowerment.

HEARTWORK EXERCISE 6: FEAR

TIP: *As you fill in the blank, think about the actions or behaviors you tend to default to when faced with the fears you've identified above. Whether withdrawing from others, overworking, seeking constant reassurance, or any other strategy, this is about recognizing how you've tried to shield yourself. Reflect on how your coping mechanisms have served you in the past and consider their effectiveness in genuinely addressing the underlying fear. This introspection is crucial to acknowledging the patterns you've created to respond to fear. They set the stage for exploring new, healthier ways to deal with your feelings.*

Fill in the blank, 'When I revisit the event, I realized in that situation, I needed _____ , but that need went unmet. *(unmet need)*

C. This sparked the fear of _____
. *(what were you afraid of happening? What did worse case scenario look like?)*

Understanding the fear behind what you've been protecting yourself from is crucial to breaking free from repetitive cycles and moving forward on your path of healing, self-discovery, and empowerment.

HEARTWORK EXERCISE 6: FEAR

TIP: *As you fill in the blank, think about the actions or behaviors you tend to default to when faced with the fears you've identified above. Whether withdrawing from others, overworking, seeking constant reassurance, or any other strategy, this is about recognizing how you've tried to shield yourself. Reflect on how your coping mechanisms have served you in the past and consider their effectiveness in genuinely addressing the underlying fear. This introspection is crucial to acknowledging the patterns you've created to respond to fear. They set the stage for exploring new, healthier ways to deal with your feelings.*

Fill in the blank, 'When I revisit the event, I realized in that situation, I needed _____ , but that need went unmet.   (*unmet need*)

C. This sparked the fear of _____

. (*what were you afraid of happening? What did worse case scenario look like?*)

Understanding the fear behind what you've been protecting yourself from is crucial to breaking free from repetitive cycles and moving forward on your path of healing, self-discovery, and empowerment.

HEARTWORK EXERCISE 6: FEAR

TIP: *As you fill in the blank, think about the actions or behaviors you tend to default to when faced with the fears you've identified above. Whether withdrawing from others, overworking, seeking constant reassurance, or any other strategy, this is about recognizing how you've tried to shield yourself. Reflect on how your coping mechanisms have served you in the past and consider their effectiveness in genuinely addressing the underlying fear. This introspection is crucial to acknowledging the patterns you've created to respond to fear. They set the stage for exploring new, healthier ways to deal with your feelings.*

Fill in the blank, 'When I revisit the event, I realized in that situation, I needed _____ , but that need went unmet. *(unmet need)*

C. This sparked the fear of _____
. *(what were you afraid of happening? What did worse case scenario look like?)*

Understanding the fear behind what you've been protecting yourself from is crucial to breaking free from repetitive cycles and moving forward on your path of healing, self-discovery, and empowerment.

HEART ~~HOME~~WORK EXERCISE 7

HEARTWORK EXERCISE 7: COPING MECHANISM

As you take a step back from Heartwork Exercise Six, you've just begun to piece together the intricate puzzle of your emotional landscape: your unmet need, the fear stemming from it, and the coping mechanism you've instinctively employed. This trio forms the subconscious engine driving your behavior, laying bare the blueprint of your reactions to life's challenges.

It's with this understanding that you can now observe how your chosen coping strategy springs into action whenever you're confronted with situations that echo these feelings and fears. It's like watching the same scene unfold every time, with your coping mechanism playing the lead role in your response. Recognizing this cycle is pivotal—it's your first step toward dismantling the automatic replay of these patterns. Every time something triggers that familiar fear, it pulls the lever on your coping mechanism. And soon, you will stand at the threshold of change, equipped with the knowledge and insight to rewrite the script. But first, let's figure out what is your coping mechanism.

Now, you're going a step further. This exercise will help you peel back another layer, revealing how you cope and why you feel the need to cope that way. Understanding this is key to breaking the cycle. It allows you to address the root of your reactions rather than just the symptoms.

So, as you prepare to fill in the blanks, be open and curious. Be ready to confront harsh truths with kindness and patience. Remember, the goal is not to judge or criticize yourself but to gain a deeper understanding of your inner workings.

Now, reflect on the fear or pain that your coping mechanism is trying to keep at bay. Is it a fear of abandonment, a deep-seated feeling of unworthiness, the pain of not feeling accepted, or something else entirely? As you fill in the second blank, allow yourself to acknowledge this core emotion honestly.

Fill in the blank, with the actions you took to protect yourself from the fear identified in Heartwork Exercise 6. Do this considering the statement you've been working on:

'When I revisit_____
_____**, I realized in that situa-**
tion, I needed   *(A. the event)*

_____**, but that need went**
unmet.   *(B. unmet need)*

This sparked the fear of _____
In response to feeling.   *(C. fear)*

this fear, I would _____
    (D. coping mechanism).

TIP: This exercise isn't just about naming your fears; it's about understanding them. By identifying the specific fear or pain you've been working so hard to avoid, you take a crucial step towards confronting and ultimately healing it. Please remember that this journey is about gentle discovery and self-compassion. Each insight you gain is a valuable piece of the puzzle in your path toward healing and growth.

HEARTWORK EXERCISE 7: COPING MECHANISM

TIP: *This exercise isn't just about naming your fears; it's about understanding them. By identifying the specific fear or pain you've been working so hard to avoid, you take a crucial step towards confronting and ultimately healing it. Please remember that this journey is about gentle discovery and self-compassion. Each insight you gain is a valuable piece of the puzzle in your path toward healing and growth.*

Fill in the blank, with the actions you took to protect yourself from the fear identified in Heartwork Exercise 6. Do this considering the statement you've been working on:

'When I revisit_____ , I realized

in that situation, I needed   (*A. the event*)

_____, but that need went

unmet.   (*B. unmet need*)

This sparked the fear of _____

In response to feeling   (*C. fear*)

this fear, I would _____

(*D. coping mechanism*).

HEARTWORK EXERCISE 7: COPING MECHANISM

TIP: *This exercise isn't just about naming your fears; it's about understanding them. By identifying the specific fear or pain you've been working so hard to avoid, you take a crucial step towards confronting and ultimately healing it. Please remember that this journey is about gentle discovery and self-compassion. Each insight you gain is a valuable piece of the puzzle in your path toward healing and growth.*

Fill in the blank, with the actions you took to protect yourself from the fear identified in Heartwork Exercise 6. Do this considering the statement you've been working on:

'When I revisit_____ , I realized in that situation, I needed   (*A. the event*)

_____ , but that need went unmet.   (*B. unmet need*)

This sparked the fear of _____
In response to feeling   (*C. fear*)

this fear, I would _____
        (*D. coping mechanism*).

HEARTWORK EXERCISE 7: COPING MECHANISM

TIP: *This exercise isn't just about naming your fears; it's about understanding them. By identifying the specific fear or pain you've been working so hard to avoid, you take a crucial step towards confronting and ultimately healing it. Please remember that this journey is about gentle discovery and self-compassion. Each insight you gain is a valuable piece of the puzzle in your path toward healing and growth.*

Fill in the blank, with the actions you took to protect yourself from the fear identified in Heartwork Exercise 6. Do this considering the statement you've been working on:

'When I revisit_____ , I realized
in that situation, I needed   (*A. the event*)

_____, but that need went
unmet.   (*B. unmet need*)

This sparked the fear of _____
In response to feeling   (*C. fear*)

this fear, I would _____
          (*D. coping mechanism*).

HEARTWORK EXERCISE 7: COPING MECHANISM

TIP: *This exercise isn't just about naming your fears; it's about understanding them. By identifying the specific fear or pain you've been working so hard to avoid, you take a crucial step towards confronting and ultimately healing it. Please remember that this journey is about gentle discovery and self-compassion. Each insight you gain is a valuable piece of the puzzle in your path toward healing and growth.*

Fill in the blank, with the actions you took to protect yourself from the fear identified in Heartwork Exercise 6. Do this considering the statement you've been working on:

'When I revisit_____ , I realized in that situation, I needed   (A. *the event*)

_____, but that need went unmet.   (B. *unmet need*)

This sparked the fear of _____
In response to feeling   (C. *fear*)

this fear, I would _____
          (D. *coping mechanism*).

HEARTWORK EXERCISE 7: COPING MECHANISM

TIP: *This exercise isn't just about naming your fears; it's about understanding them. By identifying the specific fear or pain you've been working so hard to avoid, you take a crucial step towards confronting and ultimately healing it. Please remember that this journey is about gentle discovery and self-compassion. Each insight you gain is a valuable piece of the puzzle in your path toward healing and growth.*

Fill in the blank, with the actions you took to protect yourself from the fear identified in Heartwork Exercise 6. Do this considering the statement you've been working on:

'When I revisit_____ , I realized
in that situation, I needed   (*A. the event*)

_____, but that need went
unmet.   (*B. unmet need*)

This sparked the fear of _____
In response to feeling   (*C. fear*)

this fear, I would _____
          (*D. coping mechanism*).

HEARTWORK EXERCISE 7: COPING MECHANISM

TIP: *This exercise isn't just about naming your fears; it's about understanding them. By identifying the specific fear or pain you've been working so hard to avoid, you take a crucial step towards confronting and ultimately healing it. Please remember that this journey is about gentle discovery and self-compassion. Each insight you gain is a valuable piece of the puzzle in your path toward healing and growth.*

Fill in the blank, with the actions you took to protect yourself from the fear identified in Heartwork Exercise 6. Do this considering the statement you've been working on:

'When I revisit_____ , I realized
in that situation, I needed   (*A. the event*)

_____, but that need went
unmet.   (*B. unmet need*)

This sparked the fear of _____
In response to feeling   (*C. fear*)

this fear, I would _____
         (*D. coping mechanism*).

HEARTWORK EXERCISE 7: COPING MECHANISM

TIP: *This exercise isn't just about naming your fears; it's about understanding them. By identifying the specific fear or pain you've been working so hard to avoid, you take a crucial step towards confronting and ultimately healing it. Please remember that this journey is about gentle discovery and self-compassion. Each insight you gain is a valuable piece of the puzzle in your path toward healing and growth.*

Fill in the blank, with the actions you took to protect yourself from the fear identified in Heartwork Exercise 6. Do this considering the statement you've been working on:

'When I revisit＿＿＿＿＿＿＿＿＿＿＿＿＿＿＿＿ , I realized
in that situation, I needed　　　　　　(*A. the event*)

＿＿＿＿＿＿＿＿＿＿＿＿＿＿＿, but that need went
unmet.　　　　(*B. unmet need*)

This sparked the fear of ＿＿＿＿＿＿＿＿＿＿＿＿
In response to feeling　　　　　(*C. fear*)

this fear, I would ＿＿＿＿＿＿＿＿＿＿＿＿
　　　　　(*D. coping mechanism*).

HEARTWORK EXERCISE 7: COPING MECHANISM

TIP: *This exercise isn't just about naming your fears; it's about understanding them. By identifying the specific fear or pain you've been working so hard to avoid, you take a crucial step towards confronting and ultimately healing it. Please remember that this journey is about gentle discovery and self-compassion. Each insight you gain is a valuable piece of the puzzle in your path toward healing and growth.*

Fill in the blank, with the actions you took to protect yourself from the fear identified in Heartwork Exercise 6. Do this considering the statement you've been working on:

'**When I revisit**_____ **, I realized in that situation, I needed** (*A. the event*)

_____, **but that need went unmet.** (*B. unmet need*)

This sparked the fear of _____
In response to feeling (*C. fear*)

this fear, I would _____
(*D. coping mechanism*).

HEARTWORK EXERCISE 7: COPING MECHANISM

TIP: *This exercise isn't just about naming your fears; it's about understanding them. By identifying the specific fear or pain you've been working so hard to avoid, you take a crucial step towards confronting and ultimately healing it. Please remember that this journey is about gentle discovery and self-compassion. Each insight you gain is a valuable piece of the puzzle in your path toward healing and growth.*

Fill in the blank, with the actions you took to protect yourself from the fear identified in Heartwork Exercise 6. Do this considering the statement you've been working on:

'When I revisit_____ , I realized
in that situation, I needed   (*A. the event*)

_____, but that need went
unmet.   (*B. unmet need*)

This sparked the fear of _____
In response to feeling   (*C. fear*)

this fear, I would _____
          (*D. coping mechanism*).

HEARTWORK EXERCISE 7: COPING MECHANISM

TIP: *This exercise isn't just about naming your fears; it's about understanding them. By identifying the specific fear or pain you've been working so hard to avoid, you take a crucial step towards confronting and ultimately healing it. Please remember that this journey is about gentle discovery and self-compassion. Each insight you gain is a valuable piece of the puzzle in your path toward healing and growth.*

Fill in the blank, with the actions you took to protect yourself from the fear identified in Heartwork Exercise 6. Do this considering the statement you've been working on:

'When I revisit_____ , I realized in that situation, I needed   (*A. the event*)

_____, but that need went unmet.   (*B. unmet need*)

This sparked the fear of _____
In response to feeling   (*C. fear*)

this fear, I would _____
       (*D. coping mechanism*).

HEARTWORK EXERCISE 7: COPING MECHANISM

TIP: *This exercise isn't just about naming your fears; it's about understanding them. By identifying the specific fear or pain you've been working so hard to avoid, you take a crucial step towards confronting and ultimately healing it. Please remember that this journey is about gentle discovery and self-compassion. Each insight you gain is a valuable piece of the puzzle in your path toward healing and growth.*

Fill in the blank, with the actions you took to protect yourself from the fear identified in Heartwork Exercise 6. Do this considering the statement you've been working on:

'When I revisit_____ , I realized
in that situation, I needed   (*A. the event*)

_____, but that need went
unmet.   (*B. unmet need*)

This sparked the fear of _____
In response to feeling   (*C. fear*)

this fear, I would _____
                    (*D. coping mechanism*).

COCOON SEASON

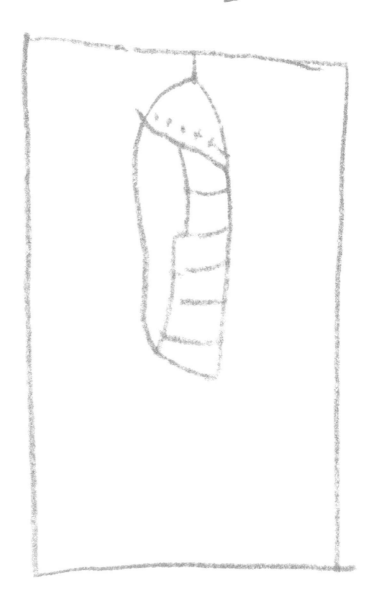

POSITIVE
THOUGHTS AND GOOD
INTENTIONS DON'T
CHANGE YOUR REALITY.
EXPANDING BEYOND
YOUR PAST, PAIN,
PATTERNS AND
PROGRAMMING DOES.

BUTTERFLY SZN

CHAPTER 7

SPROUTING

THE JOURNEY OF TRANSFORMATION

Much like a caterpillar completely transforms inside its cocoon and turns to goo before becoming a butterfly, in this chapter, you, too, will go through a profound and internal unraveling that mirrors the cocooning process. This chapter is your cocoon phase.

Those coping mechanisms you've been holding onto? They've had their day! Now, you'll look at how they've impacted your self-perception and how you interact with the world. This is your opportunity to understand how these once protective mechanisms might now stunt your growth and keep you unfulfilled.

The beauty is in the transformation. Through these heartwork exercises, you'll see the bigger picture. It will be like stepping back and seeing the whole garden, not just the individual flowers. You'll reflect on how being 'planted' in environments, places you didn't choose, has shaped who you are. While you can't change where we were planted, you can decide where you grow from here.

So, as you gear up to break through the soil and reach for the sunlight, remember that your transformation is a deliberate and empowered rebirth into who you were always meant to be. This chapter doesn't just summarize your learnings; it shines a light on your path forward, inviting you to grow in directions you never imagined possible. It's here that you transform the suffering of your cocoon season into your empowered butterfly season. Here, you lay the foundation for your renewed sense of self, ready for the growth ahead. That is the beauty of your transformation.

THIS
TRANSFORMATION
IS A DELIBERATE
AND EMPOWERED
REBIRTH INTO WHO
I WAS ALWAYS
MEANT TO BE.

BUTTERFLY SZN

HEART

~~HOME~~WORK EXERCISE 8

HEARTWORK EXERCISE 8: THE CONSEQUENCES

As the magic of unlearning to relearn unfolds, you will continue sitting with the coping mechanisms you've identified and understand their ripple effects. It's like peeling back layers to see what you do to feel safe, why, and what it leads to.

In the following exercise, you will focus on the consequences of your coping mechanisms. Think of your strategies as your go-to tools for protection, shaped by underlying fears and established patterns from past events. While they might offer temporary safety, they also come with side effects, symptoms that appear in your life every time you lean on them.

So, let's get to the heart of it. Grasping the consequences of your coping mechanisms shines a light on what you bring into your life, often without even realizing it. It's like getting a clear picture that, in trying to meet your needs, you might be taking a detour that leads you further away from where you intended to go. This insight helps you spot the gap between what you hope to achieve each time you fall back on these patterns and what actually happens. It's a wake-up call to show you that there's a mismatch between your desired outcomes and the actual results of your actions.

Fill in the Blank:

TIP: As you explore the consequences of your coping mechanisms, consider it your moment to connect the dots between your intention and the actual impact of your mechanism. Recognizing the gap between what you aim for and your achievement is a game-changer. It nudges you to consider alternative routes that will probably lead you closer to your genuine needs without unintended detours. Keep an open mind—you're mapping out a more intentional path for your journey.

When I use my coping mechanism of _____
, the consequence(s) that typically follows is

HEARTWORK EXERCISE 8: THE CONSEQUENCES

TIP: *As you explore the consequences of your coping mechanisms, consider it your moment to connect the dots between your intention and the actual impact of your mechanism. Recognizing the gap between what you aim for and your achievement is a game-changer. It nudges you to consider alternative routes that will probably lead you closer to your genuine needs without unintended detours. Keep an open mind—you're mapping out a more intentional path for your journey.*

Fill in the Blank:

D.   When I use my coping mechanism of _____, the consequence(s) that typically follows is

HEARTWORK EXERCISE 8: THE CONSEQUENCES

TIP: *As you explore the consequences of your coping mechanisms, consider it your moment to connect the dots between your intention and the actual impact of your mechanism. Recognizing the gap between what you aim for and your achievement is a game-changer. It nudges you to consider alternative routes that will probably lead you closer to your genuine needs without unintended detours. Keep an open mind—you're mapping out a more intentional path for your journey.*

Fill in the Blank:

D.   When I use my coping mechanism of _____, the consequence(s) that typically follows is

HEARTWORK EXERCISE 8: THE CONSEQUENCES

TIP: *As you explore the consequences of your coping mechanisms, consider it your moment to connect the dots between your intention and the actual impact of your mechanism. Recognizing the gap between what you aim for and your achievement is a game-changer. It nudges you to consider alternative routes that will probably lead you closer to your genuine needs without unintended detours. Keep an open mind—you're mapping out a more intentional path for your journey.*

Fill in the Blank:

D.   When I use my coping mechanism of _____, the consequence(s) that typically follows is

HEARTWORK EXERCISE 8: THE CONSEQUENCES

TIP: *As you explore the consequences of your coping mechanisms, consider it your moment to connect the dots between your intention and the actual impact of your mechanism. Recognizing the gap between what you aim for and your achievement is a game-changer. It nudges you to consider alternative routes that will probably lead you closer to your genuine needs without unintended detours. Keep an open mind—you're mapping out a more intentional path for your journey.*

Fill in the Blank:

D.   When I use my coping mechanism of _____, the consequence(s) that typically follows is

HEARTWORK EXERCISE 8: THE CONSEQUENCES

TIP: *As you explore the consequences of your coping mechanisms, consider it your moment to connect the dots between your intention and the actual impact of your mechanism. Recognizing the gap between what you aim for and your achievement is a game-changer. It nudges you to consider alternative routes that will probably lead you closer to your genuine needs without unintended detours. Keep an open mind—you're mapping out a more intentional path for your journey.*

Fill in the Blank:

D.   When I use my coping mechanism of _____, the consequence(s) that typically follows is

HEARTWORK EXERCISE 8: THE CONSEQUENCES

TIP: As you explore the consequences of your coping mechanisms, consider it your moment to connect the dots between your intention and the actual impact of your mechanism. Recognizing the gap between what you aim for and your achievement is a game-changer. It nudges you to consider alternative routes that will probably lead you closer to your genuine needs without unintended detours. Keep an open mind—you're mapping out a more intentional path for your journey.

Fill in the Blank:

D.   When I use my coping mechanism of _____, the consequence(s) that typically follows is

HEARTWORK EXERCISE 8: THE CONSEQUENCES

TIP: *As you explore the consequences of your coping mechanisms, consider it your moment to connect the dots between your intention and the actual impact of your mechanism. Recognizing the gap between what you aim for and your achievement is a game-changer. It nudges you to consider alternative routes that will probably lead you closer to your genuine needs without unintended detours. Keep an open mind—you're mapping out a more intentional path for your journey.*

Fill in the Blank:

D.   When I use my coping mechanism of _____, the consequence(s) that typically follows is

HEARTWORK EXERCISE 8: THE CONSEQUENCES

TIP: *As you explore the consequences of your coping mechanisms, consider it your moment to connect the dots between your intention and the actual impact of your mechanism. Recognizing the gap between what you aim for and your achievement is a game-changer. It nudges you to consider alternative routes that will probably lead you closer to your genuine needs without unintended detours. Keep an open mind—you're mapping out a more intentional path for your journey.*

Fill in the Blank:

D.   When I use my coping mechanism of _____, the consequence(s) that typically follows is

HEARTWORK EXERCISE 8: THE CONSEQUENCES

TIP: *As you explore the consequences of your coping mechanisms, consider it your moment to connect the dots between your intention and the actual impact of your mechanism. Recognizing the gap between what you aim for and your achievement is a game-changer. It nudges you to consider alternative routes that will probably lead you closer to your genuine needs without unintended detours. Keep an open mind—you're mapping out a more intentional path for your journey.*

Fill in the Blank:

D.   When I use my coping mechanism of _____, the consequence(s) that typically follows is

HEARTWORK EXERCISE 8: THE CONSEQUENCES

TIP: *As you explore the consequences of your coping mechanisms, consider it your moment to connect the dots between your intention and the actual impact of your mechanism. Recognizing the gap between what you aim for and your achievement is a game-changer. It nudges you to consider alternative routes that will probably lead you closer to your genuine needs without unintended detours. Keep an open mind—you're mapping out a more intentional path for your journey.*

Fill in the Blank:

D.   When I use my coping mechanism of _____, the consequence(s) that typically follows is

HEARTWORK EXERCISE 8: THE CONSEQUENCES

TIP: *As you explore the consequences of your coping mechanisms, consider it your moment to connect the dots between your intention and the actual impact of your mechanism. Recognizing the gap between what you aim for and your achievement is a game-changer. It nudges you to consider alternative routes that will probably lead you closer to your genuine needs without unintended detours. Keep an open mind—you're mapping out a more intentional path for your journey.*

Fill in the Blank:

D.   When I use my coping mechanism of _____, the consequence(s) that typically follows is

I'M
UNLEARNING
OLD BEHAVIORS
AND BECOMING
ALIGNED
WITH WHO
I WANT TO BE.

BUTTERFLY SZN

HEART
~~HOME~~WORK EXERCISE 9

HEARTWORK EXERCISE 9: THE CULMINATION

Heading into Heartwork Exercise Nine, let's pause for a second to appreciate the ground we've covered. You've been stacking these exercises like bricks, each one revealing more about the person you are and the person you're becoming. You've been piecing together the narrative of your past, pinpointing the fears and needs born from those experiences, and examining how you've been navigating them. Now, it's time to lay it all out on the flower diagram provided below, offering you a comprehensive overview of how these elements intertwine in your life.

This exercise uses your responses from the heartwork exercises above to visually represent these elements. Think of it as constructing a flower, not just any flower, but one representing the parts of your life you want to change. The flower's roots symbolize the first event, the underlying fear, and the unmet need, elements hidden beneath the surface but fundamental to your growth. The stem represents your coping mechanisms, the ways you've held yourself together through your challenges. The petals represent the consequences of your old mechanisms, the visible outcomes you're ready to reassess.

This visual exercise aims to spark that "aha" moment when you see what needs shaking up and empower you to move toward the changes you want to see in your life.

Using your answers from the fill-in-the-blank exercises above, transfer each response to the corresponding label on the flower drawing (see corresponding page numbers below):

A. event, p. 28

B. unmet need, p. 37

C. fear, p. 44

D. coping mechanism, p. 48

E. consiquences, p. 58

TIP: *As you examine your completed flower, let it guide you into a moment of reflection. Ask yourself: What insights emerge as I view this visual representation of my journey? Consider how the roots—your events, fears, and unmet needs—have nourished the stem and petals, shaping the coping mechanisms and their consequences. Observing your flower, identify one aspect you want to transform. This exercise is more than a reflection; it's an opportunity to pinpoint actionable steps toward growth and healing inspired by your flower's story.*

HEARTWORK EXERCISE 9: THE CULMINATION

Using your answers from the fill-in-the-blank exercises above, transfer each response to the corresponding label on the flower drawing:

TIP: As you examine your completed flower, let it guide you into a moment of reflection. Ask yourself: What insights emerge as I view this visual representation of my journey? Consider how the roots—your events, fears, and unmet needs—have nourished the stem and petals, shaping the coping mechanisms and their consequences. Observing your flower, identify one aspect you want to transform. This exercise is more than a reflection; it's an opportunity to pinpoint actionable steps toward growth and healing inspired by your flower's story.

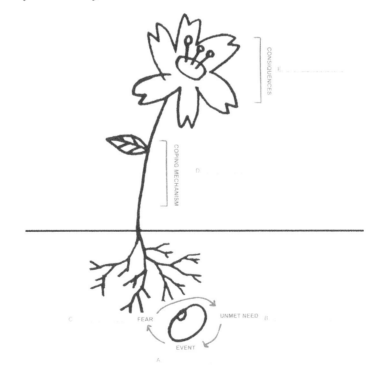

HEARTWORK EXERCISE 9: THE CULMINATION

Using your answers from the fill-in-the-blank exercises above, transfer each response to the corresponding label on the flower drawing:

TIP: As you examine your completed flower, let it guide you into a moment of reflection. Ask yourself: What insights emerge as I view this visual representation of my journey? Consider how the roots—your events, fears, and unmet needs—have nourished the stem and petals, shaping the coping mechanisms and their consequences. Observing your flower, identify one aspect you want to transform. This exercise is more than a reflection; it's an opportunity to pinpoint actionable steps toward growth and healing inspired by your flower's story.

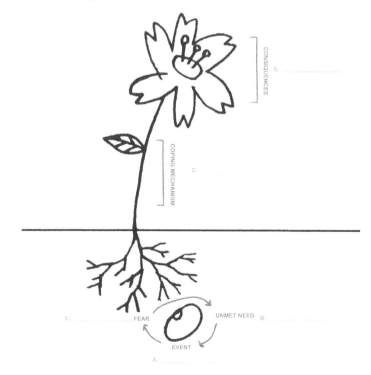

HEARTWORK EXERCISE 9: THE CULMINATION

Using your answers from the fill-in-the-blank exercises above, transfer each response to the corresponding label on the flower drawing:

TIP: *As you examine your completed flower, let it guide you into a moment of reflection. Ask yourself: What insights emerge as I view this visual representation of my journey? Consider how the roots—your events, fears, and unmet needs—have nourished the stem and petals, shaping the coping mechanisms and their consequences. Observing your flower, identify one aspect you want to transform. This exercise is more than a reflection; it's an opportunity to pinpoint actionable steps toward growth and healing inspired by your flower's story.*

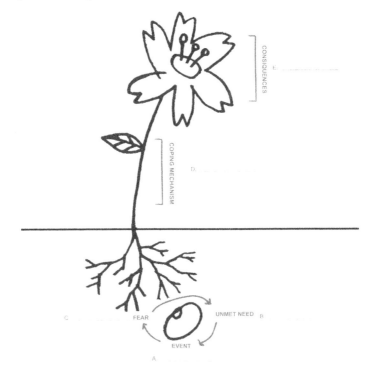

HEARTWORK EXERCISE 9: THE CULMINATION

Using your answers from the fill-in-the-blank exercises above, transfer each response to the corresponding label on the flower drawing:

TIP: *As you examine your completed flower, let it guide you into a moment of reflection. Ask yourself: What insights emerge as I view this visual representation of my journey? Consider how the roots—your events, fears, and unmet needs—have nourished the stem and petals, shaping the coping mechanisms and their consequences. Observing your flower, identify one aspect you want to transform. This exercise is more than a reflection; it's an opportunity to pinpoint actionable steps toward growth and healing inspired by your flower's story.*

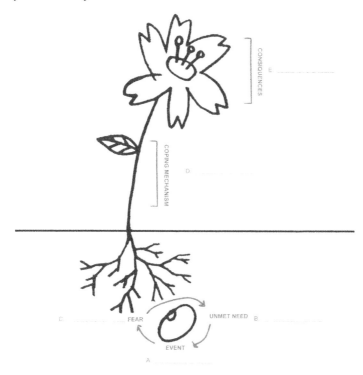

HEARTWORK EXERCISE 9: THE CULMINATION

Using your answers from the fill-in-the-blank exercises above, transfer each response to the corresponding label on the flower drawing:

TIP: As you examine your completed flower, let it guide you into a moment of reflection. Ask yourself: What insights emerge as I view this visual representation of my journey? Consider how the roots—your events, fears, and unmet needs—have nourished the stem and petals, shaping the coping mechanisms and their consequences. Observing your flower, identify one aspect you want to transform. This exercise is more than a reflection; it's an opportunity to pinpoint actionable steps toward growth and healing inspired by your flower's story.

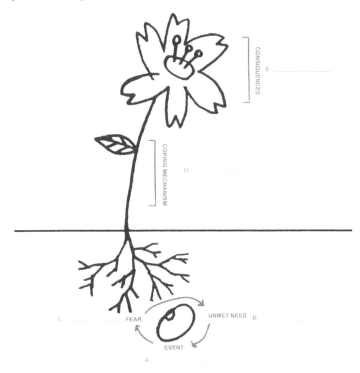

HEARTWORK EXERCISE 9: THE CULMINATION

Using your answers from the fill-in-the-blank exercises above, transfer each response to the corresponding label on the flower drawing:

TIP: As you examine your completed flower, let it guide you into a moment of reflection. Ask yourself: What insights emerge as I view this visual representation of my journey? Consider how the roots—your events, fears, and unmet needs—have nourished the stem and petals, shaping the coping mechanisms and their consequences. Observing your flower, identify one aspect you want to transform. This exercise is more than a reflection; it's an opportunity to pinpoint actionable steps toward growth and healing inspired by your flower's story.

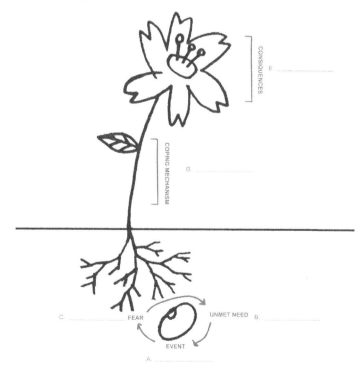

HEARTWORK EXERCISE 9: THE CULMINATION

Using your answers from the fill-in-the-blank exercises above, transfer each response to the corresponding label on the flower drawing:

TIP: As you examine your completed flower, let it guide you into a moment of reflection. Ask yourself: What insights emerge as I view this visual representation of my journey? Consider how the roots—your events, fears, and unmet needs—have nourished the stem and petals, shaping the coping mechanisms and their consequences. Observing your flower, identify one aspect you want to transform. This exercise is more than a reflection; it's an opportunity to pinpoint actionable steps toward growth and healing inspired by your flower's story.

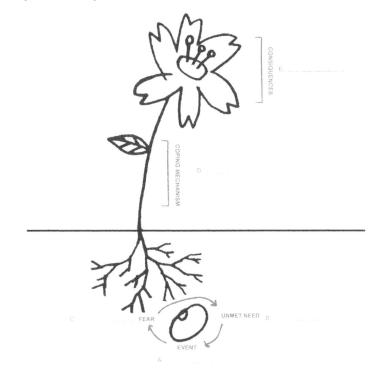

HEARTWORK EXERCISE 9: THE CULMINATION

Using your answers from the fill-in-the-blank exercises above, transfer each response to the corresponding label on the flower drawing:

TIP: *As you examine your completed flower, let it guide you into a moment of reflection. Ask yourself: What insights emerge as I view this visual representation of my journey? Consider how the roots—your events, fears, and unmet needs—have nourished the stem and petals, shaping the coping mechanisms and their consequences. Observing your flower, identify one aspect you want to transform. This exercise is more than a reflection; it's an opportunity to pinpoint actionable steps toward growth and healing inspired by your flower's story.*

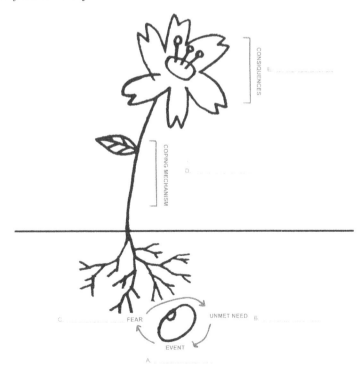

HEARTWORK EXERCISE 9: THE CULMINATION

Using your answers from the fill-in-the-blank exercises above, transfer each response to the corresponding label on the flower drawing:

TIP: As you examine your completed flower, let it guide you into a moment of reflection. Ask yourself: What insights emerge as I view this visual representation of my journey? Consider how the roots—your events, fears, and unmet needs—have nourished the stem and petals, shaping the coping mechanisms and their consequences. Observing your flower, identify one aspect you want to transform. This exercise is more than a reflection; it's an opportunity to pinpoint actionable steps toward growth and healing inspired by your flower's story.

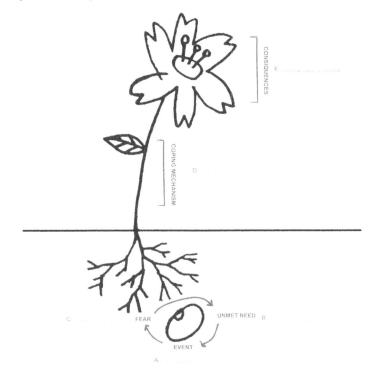

HEARTWORK EXERCISE 9: THE CULMINATION

Using your answers from the fill-in-the-blank exercises above, transfer each response to the corresponding label on the flower drawing:

TIP: *As you examine your completed flower, let it guide you into a moment of reflection. Ask yourself: What insights emerge as I view this visual representation of my journey? Consider how the roots—your events, fears, and unmet needs—have nourished the stem and petals, shaping the coping mechanisms and their consequences. Observing your flower, identify one aspect you want to transform. This exercise is more than a reflection; it's an opportunity to pinpoint actionable steps toward growth and healing inspired by your flower's story.*

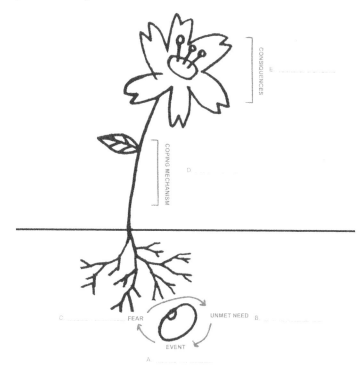

HEARTWORK EXERCISE 9: THE CULMINATION

Using your answers from the fill-in-the-blank exercises above, transfer each response to the corresponding label on the flower drawing:

TIP: As you examine your completed flower, let it guide you into a moment of reflection. Ask yourself: What insights emerge as I view this visual representation of my journey? Consider how the roots—your events, fears, and unmet needs—have nourished the stem and petals, shaping the coping mechanisms and their consequences. Observing your flower, identify one aspect you want to transform. This exercise is more than a reflection; it's an opportunity to pinpoint actionable steps toward growth and healing inspired by your flower's story.

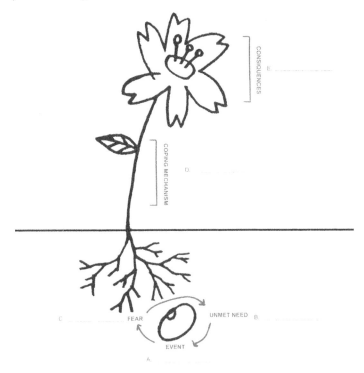

CHAPTER 8

BREAKING THE CYLE

TRANSFORMING HURT INTO HEALING

Reflecting on the journey you've embarked upon with the heartwork exercises, particularly as you fill out the flower diagram, it's essential to recognize a deeper cycle that often goes unnoticed. This cycle begins when actions from others leave us with unmet needs, a common thread in the tapestry of human relationships. These unmet needs, born from moments where we felt let down or unsupported, become the blueprint for how we might unconsciously respond in similar situations.

In a nuanced turn of events, the strategies we adopt to fulfill these needs can sometimes mirror the actions that initially caused our discomfort or pain. It's not about assigning blame but understanding a natural, albeit complex, human behavior pattern. When we act from a place of unmet need, without conscious healing, we may inadvertently create experiences for others that resemble the discomfort we ourselves have faced. This cycle—a reflection of seeking fulfillment in ways we've known, even if they're flawed—highlights the interconnectedness of our actions and their broader impact.

At this point in your journey, it's crucial to pause for a moment of reflection. Can you see the parallels between the actions that led to your unmet needs and the actions you find yourself taking in similar situations? This moment of realization is profound, illuminating how the cycle of unmet needs and our responses to them can perpetuate a pattern we never intended to repeat. Recognizing these similarities is a vital step in the journey toward breaking this cycle.

The significance of recognizing and breaking this cycle extends beyond personal healing. It's about altering the legacy of our interactions, transforming them from patterns that replicate past wounds to ones that foster understanding and support. By engaging in heartwork, you're not only navigating a path to personal transformation but also contributing to a shift in how we all impact each other.

This transformative work serves a dual purpose: it is a journey towards healing the parts of ourselves that have been hurt, and it's a conscious effort to ensure that our actions become sources of positivity rather than perpetuation of past patterns. Through this process, you're invited to explore new ways of meeting your needs that enrich rather than echo past experiences, setting a foundation for interactions that uplift both yourself and those around you.

Thus, the heartwork you're doing is invaluable. It's a step towards individual freedom and a contribution to a collective environment where understanding, rather than unintentional repetition of past events, guides our actions. This is the essence of transforming not only your life but also playing a part in healing the broader tapestry of human connections.

TRUST.
YOU'LL LEAVE
THE COCOON A
DIFFERENT
PERSON.

BUTTERFLY SZN

CHAPTER 9

REPLANTING

THE JOURNEY OF TRANSFORMATION

Are you ready to replant your flower in fertile ground using what's held you back to proactively shape your future? The following heartwork exercises will help you discover what genuinely nourishes you. They will allow you to identify the 'sun' and 'water' your flower needs. Just as plants need sun and water to thrive, you need a balance of external support (your community is the sun) and internal sustenance (your self-care is the water).

Both elements are essential. The 'sun' of community nourishment and the 'water' of self-care create the ideal growth conditions. This exercise is about finding the right balance that allows you to thrive.

So, here is the flower exercise again. But this time, you can choose where this flower, representing your new coping mechanisms and growth, is planted. You're in control of selecting an environment that meets your needs and leads to positive outcomes in your life. Here's to planting the seeds of change and watching them bloom into a healthier, happier you.

HEART
~~HOME~~WORK EXERCISE 10

HEARTWORK EXERCISE 10: EMPOWERMENT

In the wake of a an event that has you reeling, what often unfolds is a journey through fear and the unveiling of unmet needs. Initially, fear takes the lead—a visceral, immediate response that your brains conjure up to protect you. This fear, deeply rooted in your instinctual fight-or-flight mechanism, serves as a guard, aiming to shield you from perceived threats and ensure your survival. It's a universal reaction, one that every person has felt at one point or another in the face of trauma.

However, as the dust settles and you begin to process this fear, another layer of your experience starts to surface: the unmet needs that the event has brought into sharp focus. These needs—whether for safety, stability, understanding, connection, or healing—often remain obscured until you've had the chance to reflect on the event and its deeper impact on your emotional and psychological state. It's during this period of reflection and understanding that you start to see the full picture, recognizing how the trauma has not only triggered fear but also highlighted areas of your life where there are significant gaps.

Understanding this sequence is crucial. Initially, fear acts as a protective barrier, a natural response designed to keep us safe. But following this, as we move through the healing process, our unmet needs emerge, demanding attention and care. It's a natural progression from an immediate protective reaction to a more profound understanding of what we need to heal and grow.

Entering Heartwork Exercise with this backdrop helps to frame our approach. The seed of this exercise represents more than just a desire to cope better; it signifies a deep-seated intention to understand and nurture our unmet needs and fears in a way that fosters growth and healing.

The seed represents your desire to develop healthier ways of dealing with life's challenges, grounded in a deep understanding of your unmet needs and fears. This Heartwork Exercise aims to help you identify and adopt healthier coping mechanisms that positively address your unmet needs.

Step 1 Reflect on Your Unmet Needs

To find a healthier coping mechanism, we need to address the seed. As a refresher, fill in your roots:

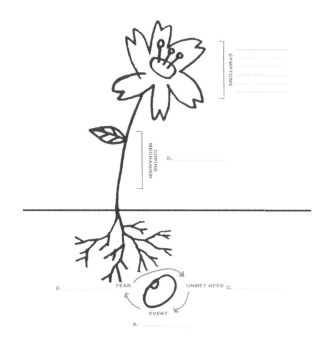

Step 2 Question for Reflection

"What positive action can I take that acknowledges and addresses my unmet need without leading to the negative consequences I've experienced before?" List healthy behaviors or actions that could serve as new coping mechanisms. These should be actions that empower you.

Step 3 Evaluate Your Options

Consider how each coping mechanism on your list might meet your unmet needs. Does it align with your positive intentions? Will it likely lead to better outcomes than your previous coping mechanism?

TIP: Remember that the most empowering person who can meet your needs is you. Reflect on activities that make you feel fulfilled and in control, and consider how these can become your go-to responses in challenging times. Finding actions that address your needs and reinforce your independence and self-worth is key. Your self-reliance is your secret garden where your resilience blooms.

Step 4 Fill In Your Coping Mechanism

Fill in your coping new mechanism below. Remember, your new coping mechanism should testify to your strength and ability to support yourself.

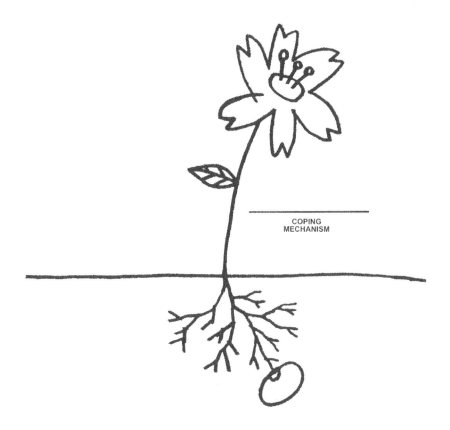

COPING
MECHANISM

HEARTWORK EXERCISE 10: EMPOWERMENT

Fill In Your Coping Mechanism

Fill in your coping new mechanism below. Remember, your new coping mechanism should testify to your strength and ability to support yourself.

TIP: Remember that the most empowering person who can meet your needs is you. Reflect on activities that make you feel fulfilled and in control, and consider how these can become your go-to responses in challenging times. Finding actions that address your needs and reinforce your independence and self-worth is key. Your self-reliance is your secret garden where your resilience blooms.

COPING
MECHANISM

HEARTWORK EXERCISE 10: EMPOWERMENT

Fill In Your Coping Mechanism

Fill in your coping new mechanism below. Remember, your new coping mechanism should testify to your strength and ability to support yourself.

TIP: *Remember that the most empowering person who can meet your needs is you. Reflect on activities that make you feel fulfilled and in control, and consider how these can become your go-to responses in challenging times. Finding actions that address your needs and reinforce your independence and self-worth is key. Your self-reliance is your secret garden where your resilience blooms.*

COPING
MECHANISM

HEARTWORK EXERCISE 10: EMPOWERMENT

Fill In Your Coping Mechanism

Fill in your coping new mechanism below. Remember, your new coping mechanism should testify to your strength and ability to support yourself.

TIP: Remember that the most empowering person who can meet your needs is you. Reflect on activities that make you feel fulfilled and in control, and consider how these can become your go-to responses in challenging times. Finding actions that address your needs and reinforce your independence and self-worth is key. Your self-reliance is your secret garden where your resilience blooms.

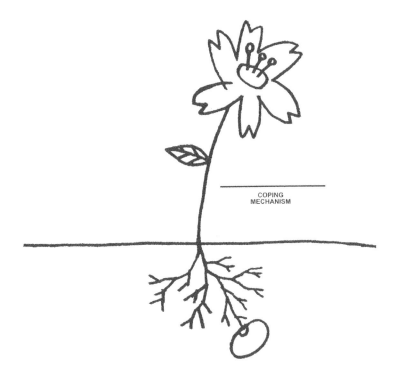

COPING
MECHANISM

HEARTWORK EXERCISE 10: EMPOWERMENT

Fill In Your Coping Mechanism

Fill in your coping new mechanism below. Remember, your new coping mechanism should testify to your strength and ability to support yourself.

TIP: *Remember that the most empowering person who can meet your needs is you. Reflect on activities that make you feel fulfilled and in control, and consider how these can become your go-to responses in challenging times. Finding actions that address your needs and reinforce your independence and self-worth is key. Your self-reliance is your secret garden where your resilience blooms.*

COPING
MECHANISM

HEARTWORK EXERCISE 10: EMPOWERMENT

Fill In Your Coping Mechanism

Fill in your coping new mechanism below. Remember, your new coping mechanism should testify to your strength and ability to support yourself.

TIP: Remember that the most empowering person who can meet your needs is you. Reflect on activities that make you feel fulfilled and in control, and consider how these can become your go-to responses in challenging times. Finding actions that address your needs and reinforce your independence and self-worth is key. Your self-reliance is your secret garden where your resilience blooms.

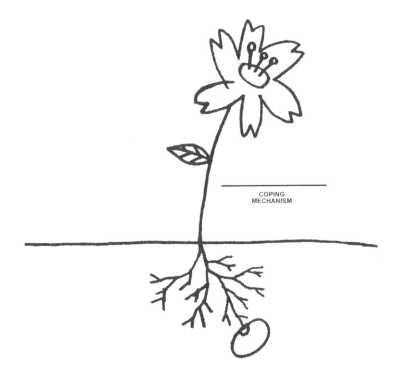

COPING
MECHANISM

HEARTWORK EXERCISE 10: EMPOWERMENT

Fill In Your Coping Mechanism

Fill in your coping new mechanism below. Remember, your new coping mechanism should testify to your strength and ability to support yourself.

TIP: Remember that the most empowering person who can meet your needs is you. Reflect on activities that make you feel fulfilled and in control, and consider how these can become your go-to responses in challenging times. Finding actions that address your needs and reinforce your independence and self-worth is key. Your self-reliance is your secret garden where your resilience blooms.

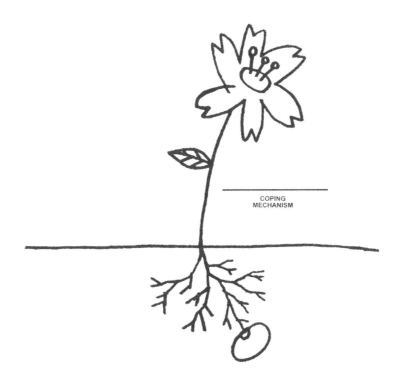

COPING
MECHANISM

HEARTWORK EXERCISE 10: EMPOWERMENT

Fill In Your Coping Mechanism

Fill in your coping new mechanism below. Remember, your new coping mechanism should testify to your strength and ability to support yourself.

TIP: Remember that the most empowering person who can meet your needs is you. Reflect on activities that make you feel fulfilled and in control, and consider how these can become your go-to responses in challenging times. Finding actions that address your needs and reinforce your independence and self-worth is key. Your self-reliance is your secret garden where your resilience blooms.

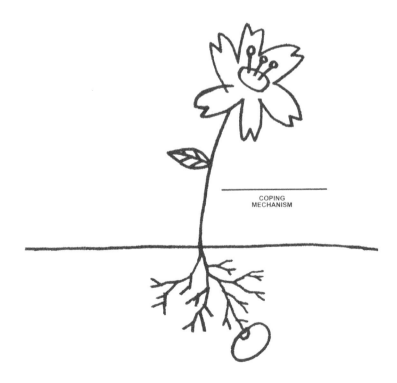

COPING
MECHANISM

HEARTWORK EXERCISE 10: EMPOWERMENT

Fill In Your Coping Mechanism

Fill in your coping new mechanism below. Remember, your new coping mechanism should testify to your strength and ability to support yourself.

TIP: Remember that the most empowering person who can meet your needs is you. Reflect on activities that make you feel fulfilled and in control, and consider how these can become your go-to responses in challenging times. Finding actions that address your needs and reinforce your independence and self-worth is key. Your self-reliance is your secret garden where your resilience blooms.

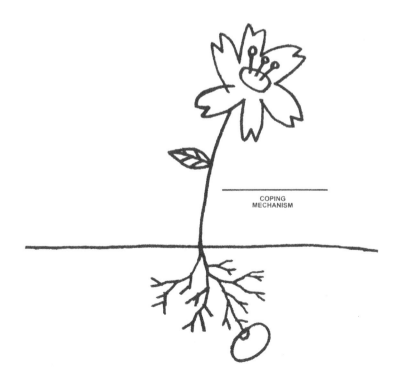

COPING
MECHANISM

HEARTWORK EXERCISE 10: EMPOWERMENT

Fill In Your Coping Mechanism

Fill in your coping new mechanism below. Remember, your new coping mechanism should testify to your strength and ability to support yourself.

TIP: Remember that the most empowering person who can meet your needs is you. Reflect on activities that make you feel fulfilled and in control, and consider how these can become your go-to responses in challenging times. Finding actions that address your needs and reinforce your independence and self-worth is key. Your self-reliance is your secret garden where your resilience blooms.

COPING
MECHANISM

HEARTWORK EXERCISE 10: EMPOWERMENT

Fill In Your Coping Mechanism

Fill in your coping new mechanism below. Remember, your new coping mechanism should testify to your strength and ability to support yourself.

TIP: Remember that the most empowering person who can meet your needs is you. Reflect on activities that make you feel fulfilled and in control, and consider how these can become your go-to responses in challenging times. Finding actions that address your needs and reinforce your independence and self-worth is key. Your self-reliance is your secret garden where your resilience blooms.

COPING
MECHANISM

HEARTWORK EXERCISE 10: EMPOWERMENT

Fill In Your Coping Mechanism

Fill in your coping new mechanism below. Remember, your new coping mechanism should testify to your strength and ability to support yourself.

TIP: *Remember that the most empowering person who can meet your needs is you. Reflect on activities that make you feel fulfilled and in control, and consider how these can become your go-to responses in challenging times. Finding actions that address your needs and reinforce your independence and self-worth is key. Your self-reliance is your secret garden where your resilience blooms.*

COPING
MECHANISM

LIFE BECOMES
BEAUTIFUL
WHEN WE
RECOGNIZE
THE BEAUTY OF
TRANSFORMATION.

BUTTERFLY SZN

HEART

~~HOME~~WORK EXERCISE 11

HEARTWORK EXERCISE 11: YOUR SUN AND WATER

You've tended to the roots and strengthened the stem. Now, it's time to bask in the sun and absorb the water that will fuel your growth. Think of the sun and water as metaphors for the external (your community) and internal (your self-care) nourishments that sustain your growth. Your 'sun' represents the community, relationships, and external support systems that energize you. Your 'water' symbolizes the self-care practices and inner resources that keep you grounded and flourishing.

 WATER
Water symbolizes the resources and self-care practices that nourish your intention and help you grow.

 SUN
The Sun represents the positive influence and support of your community.

The goal here is to help you pinpoint how the sun, the external support, looks in your life and identify your water, the internal sustenance that nurtures your personal growth. By recognizing these sources, you can actively seek them out and integrate them into your daily life,

Step 1 Define Your Sun

Reflect on the people, communities, and environments that provide you with energy, encouragement, and motivation. Write down these sources of sun and describe how they can contribute to your sense of empowerment.

HEARTWORK EXERCISE 11: YOUR SUN AND WATER

Step 1 Define Your Sun

Reflect on the people, communities, and environments that provide you with energy, encouragement, and motivation. Write down these sources of sun and describe how they can contribute to your sense of empowerment.

HEARTWORK EXERCISE 11: YOUR SUN AND WATER

Step 2 Explore Your Water

Turn your focus inward and consider the self-care practices that maintain your internal balance and peace. List the activities and habits that replenish your inner strength and keep you grounded.

HEARTWORK EXERCISE 11: YOUR SUN AND WATER

Step 3 Integrate Your Support

Use your lists of sun and water to help you think about how to incorporate them into your daily life. Plan actionable steps to seek out your sun and regularly engage in your water activities.

Tip: *To uncover your sun and water, think about when you've felt at your best. What were you doing? Who were you with? These are clues to what genuinely sustains you. Your sun might be the encouragement from friends, while your water could be those quiet moments of meditation or a creative hobby.*

HEARTWORK EXERCISE 11: YOUR SUN AND WATER

Step 3 Integrate Your Support

Use your lists of sun and water to help you think about how to incorporate them into your daily life. Plan actionable steps to seek out your sun and regularly engage in your water activities.

Tip: *To uncover your sun and water, think about when you've felt at your best. What were you doing? Who were you with? These are clues to what genuinely sustains you. Your sun might be the encouragement from friends, while your water could be those quiet moments of meditation or a creative hobby.*

HEARTWORK EXERCISE 11: YOUR SUN AND WATER

Step 3 Integrate Your Support

Use your lists of sun and water to help you think about how to incorporate them into your daily life. Plan actionable steps to seek out your sun and regularly engage in your water activities.

Tip: *To uncover your sun and water, think about when you've felt at your best. What were you doing? Who were you with? These are clues to what genuinely sustains you. Your sun might be the encouragement from friends, while your water could be those quiet moments of meditation or a creative hobby.*

HEARTWORK EXERCISE 11: YOUR SUN AND WATER

Step 3 Integrate Your Support

Use your lists of sun and water to help you think about how to incorporate them into your daily life. Plan actionable steps to seek out your sun and regularly engage in your water activities.

Tip: *To uncover your sun and water, think about when you've felt at your best. What were you doing? Who were you with? These are clues to what genuinely sustains you. Your sun might be the encouragement from friends, while your water could be those quiet moments of meditation or a creative hobby.*

HEARTWORK EXERCISE 11: YOUR SUN AND WATER

Step 3 Integrate Your Support

Use your lists of sun and water to help you think about how to incorporate them into your daily life. Plan actionable steps to seek out your sun and regularly engage in your water activities.

Tip: *To uncover your sun and water, think about when you've felt at your best. What were you doing? Who were you with? These are clues to what genuinely sustains you. Your sun might be the encouragement from friends, while your water could be those quiet moments of meditation or a creative hobby.*

HEARTWORK EXERCISE 11: YOUR SUN AND WATER

Step 3 Integrate Your Support

Use your lists of sun and water to help you think about how to incorporate them into your daily life. Plan actionable steps to seek out your sun and regularly engage in your water activities.

Tip: *To uncover your sun and water, think about when you've felt at your best. What were you doing? Who were you with? These are clues to what genuinely sustains you. Your sun might be the encouragement from friends, while your water could be those quiet moments of meditation or a creative hobby.*

HEARTWORK EXERCISE 11: YOUR SUN AND WATER

Step 3 Integrate Your Support

Use your lists of sun and water to help you think about how to incorporate them into your daily life. Plan actionable steps to seek out your sun and regularly engage in your water activities.

Tip: *To uncover your sun and water, think about when you've felt at your best. What were you doing? Who were you with? These are clues to what genuinely sustains you. Your sun might be the encouragement from friends, while your water could be those quiet moments of meditation or a creative hobby.*

HEARTWORK EXERCISE 11: YOUR SUN AND WATER

Step 3 Integrate Your Support

Use your lists of sun and water to help you think about how to incorporate them into your daily life. Plan actionable steps to seek out your sun and regularly engage in your water activities.

Tip: *To uncover your sun and water, think about when you've felt at your best. What were you doing? Who were you with? These are clues to what genuinely sustains you. Your sun might be the encouragement from friends, while your water could be those quiet moments of meditation or a creative hobby.*

HEARTWORK EXERCISE 11: YOUR SUN AND WATER

Step 3 Integrate Your Support

Use your lists of sun and water to help you think about how to incorporate them into your daily life. Plan actionable steps to seek out your sun and regularly engage in your water activities.

Tip: *To uncover your sun and water, think about when you've felt at your best. What were you doing? Who were you with? These are clues to what genuinely sustains you. Your sun might be the encouragement from friends, while your water could be those quiet moments of meditation or a creative hobby.*

HEARTWORK EXERCISE 11: YOUR SUN AND WATER

Step 3 Integrate Your Support

Use your lists of sun and water to help you think about how to incorporate them into your daily life. Plan actionable steps to seek out your sun and regularly engage in your water activities.

Tip: *To uncover your sun and water, think about when you've felt at your best. What were you doing? Who were you with? These are clues to what genuinely sustains you. Your sun might be the encouragement from friends, while your water could be those quiet moments of meditation or a creative hobby.*

HEARTWORK EXERCISE 11: YOUR SUN AND WATER

Step 3 Integrate Your Support

Use your lists of sun and water to help you think about how to incorporate them into your daily life. Plan actionable steps to seek out your sun and regularly engage in your water activities.

Tip: *To uncover your sun and water, think about when you've felt at your best. What were you doing? Who were you with? These are clues to what genuinely sustains you. Your sun might be the encouragement from friends, while your water could be those quiet moments of meditation or a creative hobby.*

BUTTERFLY SEASON

IF YOU SPEND TIME CHASING
BUTTERFLIES, THEY'LL FLY AWAY.

BUT IF YOU SPEND TIME MAKING
A BEAUTIFUL GARDEN, THE
BUTTERFLIES WILL COME TO YOU.

WHEN YOU FOCUS ON IMPROVING
YOURSELF, EVERYTHING YOU WANT
WILL COME TO YOU.

WE ATTRACT BASED ON WHO WE
ARE, NOT WHAT WE WANT.

DON'T CHASE, ATTRACT.

BUTTERFLY SZN

CHAPTER 10

FLOWERING

BLOOM WHERE <u>YOU</u> PLANT

Now, you've consciously chosen where you want to be planted. You've sought an environment with just the right amount of sun and water, the essential elements you need to thrive. This isn't about being in a random place in the garden of life but selecting the spot where you know you'll flourish best. With the perfect balance of external support and internal nourishment, it's time to bloom where you've planted yourself.

Welcome to the final phase of your transformation: Butterfly Season. This chapter marks a significant milestone where the wisdom you've gained from a deeper understanding of yourself becomes the key to breaking free from patterns that have kept you circling the same issues. Butterfly Season is when the new version of you takes autonomy over your life and creates lasting change.

Embodying Butterfly Season requires consistency. Genuine transformation unfolds over time. It's a process, not a one-time event. Breaking old patterns isn't easy; it demands dedication and commitment. With this book, you've journeyed through the self-awareness of Caterpillar Season, immersed yourself in the reflective depths of Cocoon Season, and now, you're ready to embody the empowerment of Butterfly Season.

This chapter's heartwork exercises aim to give you proactive tools for your embodiment phase. It's about moving beyond understanding into well-being and living the changes you've worked hard to uncover and understand. In this phase, your transformation becomes visible to you and the world around you. It's where the internal shifts manifest into external expressions, and the beauty of your growth is revealed in full color.

As you do the heartwork exercises, approach them with an open heart. This is your time to shine and show up for yourself in ways you might never have thought possible. Commit to the consistency required to make lasting change, and remember, every effort you put in is a step toward the life you've always wanted.

RIGHT NOW,
MY MOST
SIGNIFICANT
ASSIGNMENT IS
TO WATER
MYSLEF.

BUTTERFLY SZN

HEART

~~HOME~~WORK EXERCISE 12

HEARTWORK EXERCISE 12: REPLANT

In this Heartwork exercise, you can redefine what each part of a flower means in the garden of your life and replant with intention.

In the previous heartwork exercises, you've come to understand the roots as initial events, fears, and needs that lay hidden but are fundamental to your growth. The stem was the support system, your coping mechanisms, and the petals were the consequences, the parts of your life ready for reevaluation.

Now, you can take those elements and transform their meanings to fuel your journey forward. The sun in your garden symbolizes your community's positive influences and support, shining down and guiding your way. Water represents your self-care practices that sustain and nourish you, your internal work that keeps you grounded and growing. Together, they create the ideal conditions for your new seeds of intention—your motivation to change—to take root.

The stem of your flower is now the embodiment of your new, healthy coping mechanisms, standing tall and strong. The petals have blossomed into the visible manifestations of these mechanisms, the positive outcomes that align with the intentions set out before them. And the roots? They signify a deep understanding of your past, giving you a stable foundation from which to rise:

SUN
The Sun represents the positive influen and support of your community

 STEM
The stem is your newly adopted health coping mechanism

 WATER
Water symbolizes the resources and self-care practices that nourish your intention and help you grow

 ROOTS
Roots signify the deep understanding your past experiences, including how events led to fears and unmet needs.

 PETALS
Petals are the visible manifestations of your healthy coping mechanism

 SEED
The seed represents your intention or motivation to change. It's the foundatio desire to cultivate healthier coping mechanisms

Step 1 Label the Roots

Below, you wil find an empty flower diagram. Fill the flower in by writing down the understanding you've gained about your past experiences that are the foundation for your growth.

Step 2 Define the Stem

Indicate your chosen healthy coping mechanism on the stem and highlight how it supports you now.

Step 3 Decorate the Petals

Describe the positive outcomes you expect from your new coping strategies around or on each petal.

Step 4 Add Sun and Water

Around your flower, illustrate your 'sun' and 'water' elements. Label them with the community support and self-care practices that will sustain your growth.

HEARTWORK EXERCISE 12: REPLANT

Tip: As you fill in this new flower diagram, consider it a map of your inner garden. Recognize that, unlike before, every part of this flower and where you're planted is your choice, symbolizing your autonomy and commitment to bloom into your best possible self. This exercise is your opportunity to visualize and plant the seeds for the vibrant new life you're creating.

HEARTWORK EXERCISE 12: REPLANT

Tip: As you fill in this new flower diagram, consider it a map of your inner garden. Recognize that, <u>unlike before</u>, every part of this flower and where you're planted is your choice, symbolizing your autonomy and commitment to bloom into your best possible self. This exercise is your opportunity to visualize and plant the seeds for the vibrant new life you're creating.

HEARTWORK EXERCISE 12: REPLANT

Tip: As you fill in this new flower diagram, consider it a map of your inner garden. Recognize that, <u>unlike before</u>, every part of this flower and where you're planted is your choice, symbolizing your autonomy and commitment to bloom into your best possible self. This exercise is your opportunity to visualize and plant the seeds for the vibrant new life you're creating.

HEARTWORK EXERCISE 12: REPLANT

Tip: As you fill in this new flower diagram, consider it a map of your inner garden. Recognize that, <u>unlike before</u>, every part of this flower and where you're planted is your choice, symbolizing your autonomy and commitment to bloom into your best possible self. This exercise is your opportunity to visualize and plant the seeds for the vibrant new life you're creating.

HEARTWORK EXERCISE 12: REPLANT

Tip: As you fill in this new flower diagram, consider it a map of your inner garden. Recognize that, unlike before, every part of this flower and where you're planted is your choice, symbolizing your autonomy and commitment to bloom into your best possible self. This exercise is your opportunity to visualize and plant the seeds for the vibrant new life you're creating.

HEARTWORK EXERCISE 12: REPLANT

Tip: As you fill in this new flower diagram, consider it a map of your inner garden. Recognize that, unlike before, every part of this flower and where you're planted is your choice, symbolizing your autonomy and commitment to bloom into your best possible self. This exercise is your opportunity to visualize and plant the seeds for the vibrant new life you're creating.

HEARTWORK EXERCISE 12: REPLANT

Tip: As you fill in this new flower diagram, consider it a map of your inner garden. Recognize that, unlike before, every part of this flower and where you're planted is your choice, symbolizing your autonomy and commitment to bloom into your best possible self. This exercise is your opportunity to visualize and plant the seeds for the vibrant new life you're creating.

HEARTWORK EXERCISE 12: REPLANT

Tip: *As you fill in this new flower diagram, consider it a map of your inner garden. Recognize that, unlike before, every part of this flower and where you're planted is your choice, symbolizing your autonomy and commitment to bloom into your best possible self. This exercise is your opportunity to visualize and plant the seeds for the vibrant new life you're creating.*

HEARTWORK EXERCISE 12: REPLANT

Tip: As you fill in this new flower diagram, consider it a map of your inner garden. Recognize that, <u>unlike before</u>, every part of this flower and where you're planted is your choice, symbolizing your autonomy and commitment to bloom into your best possible self. This exercise is your opportunity to visualize and plant the seeds for the vibrant new life you're creating.

HEARTWORK EXERCISE 12: REPLANT

Tip: As you fill in this new flower diagram, consider it a map of your inner garden. Recognize that, <u>unlike before</u>, every part of this flower and where you're planted is your choice, symbolizing your autonomy and commitment to bloom into your best possible self. This exercise is your opportunity to visualize and plant the seeds for the vibrant new life you're creating.

HEARTWORK EXERCISE 12: REPLANT

Tip: As you fill in this new flower diagram, consider it a map of your inner garden. Recognize that, unlike before, every part of this flower and where you're planted is your choice, symbolizing your autonomy and commitment to bloom into your best possible self. This exercise is your opportunity to visualize and plant the seeds for the vibrant new life you're creating.

THE REAL
FLEX IS
SAVING
YOUR DAMN
SELF.

BUTTERFLY SZN

HEART ~~HOME~~WORK EXERCISE 13

HEARTWORK EXERCISE 13: EMBODY

In the Butterfly SZN journal's final exercise, it's time to consolidate everything you've learned about yourself and your patterns. Breaking free from deeply ingrained reactions is a challenge. But with the right approach, you can transform these automatic responses into empowering actions.

This heartwork exercise aims to build your confidence in handling future scenarios that might trigger your coping mechanism. By intentionally crafting responses using your new self-reliant coping mechanism, you'll set the stage for positive outcomes when faced with similar triggers.

Step 1 Identify Potential Triggers

Reflect on scenarios that might trigger your old patterns. Write them down as clearly as possible.

Step 2 Craft New Responses

For each scenario, outline a constructive response that employs your new coping mechanism. How will you act differently? Write your responses as scripts (what you will say or do) or affirmations.

Step 3 Mental Rehearsal

Visualize yourself in these situations, responding with your new coping mechanism. Mentally rehearse the scenarios and feel the power of handling them proactively.

Step 4 Practice and Prepare

Commit to practicing these new responses in your daily life. Start small, with manageable situations, and gradually build up your confidence.

Step 6 Reflection and Adjustment

After attempting your new responses, reflect on how they felt and the outcomes. Adjust your scripts and support systems if you need to.

HEARTWORK EXERCISE 13: EMBODY

TIP: Remember, the key to success is preparation. A ready-made response you've mentally rehearsed can make all the difference when old patterns threaten to resurface. Your preparedness and the systems you put in place are your safety net, ensuring that you're not just reacting but actively shaping your life with your newfound resilience and autonomy.

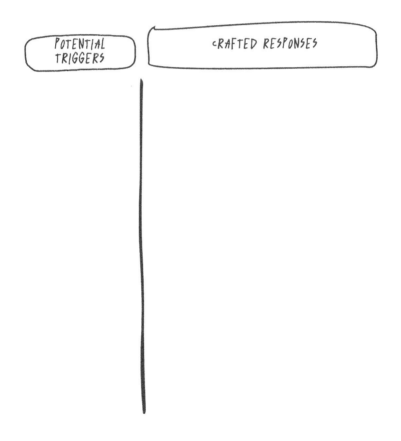

HEARTWORK EXERCISE 13: EMBODY

TIP: Remember, the key to success is preparation. A ready-made response you've mentally rehearsed can make all the difference when old patterns threaten to resurface. Your preparedness and the systems you put in place are your safety net, ensuring that you're not just reacting but actively shaping your life with your newfound resilience and autonomy.

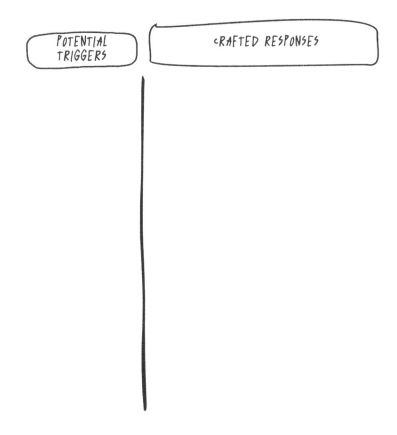

HEARTWORK EXERCISE 13: EMBODY

TIP: Remember, the key to success is preparation. A ready-made response you've mentally rehearsed can make all the difference when old patterns threaten to resurface. Your preparedness and the systems you put in place are your safety net, ensuring that you're not just reacting but actively shaping your life with your newfound resilience and autonomy.

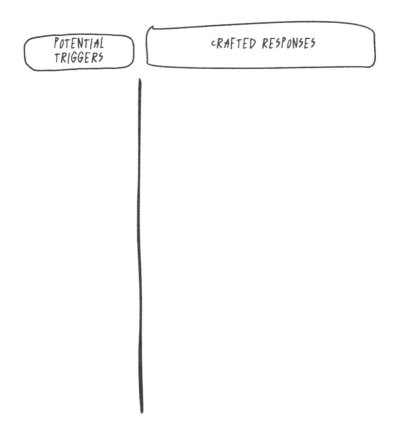

HEARTWORK EXERCISE 13: EMBODY

TIP: Remember, the key to success is preparation. A ready-made response you've mentally rehearsed can make all the difference when old patterns threaten to resurface. Your preparedness and the systems you put in place are your safety net, ensuring that you're not just reacting but actively shaping your life with your newfound resilience and autonomy.

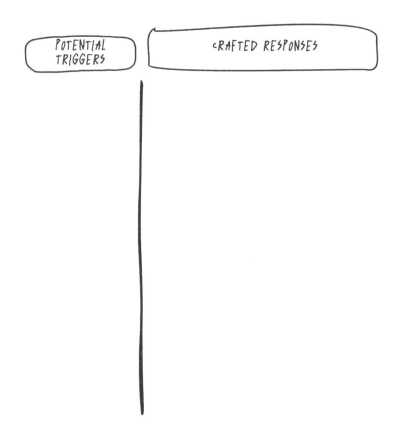

HEARTWORK EXERCISE 13: EMBODY

TIP: Remember, the key to success is preparation. A ready-made response you've mentally rehearsed can make all the difference when old patterns threaten to resurface. Your preparedness and the systems you put in place are your safety net, ensuring that you're not just reacting but actively shaping your life with your newfound resilience and autonomy.

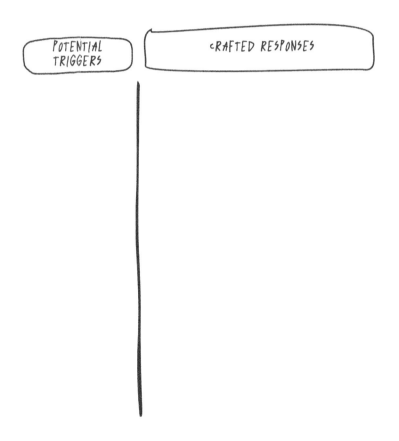

HEARTWORK EXERCISE 13: EMBODY

TIP: Remember, the key to success is preparation. A ready-made response you've mentally rehearsed can make all the difference when old patterns threaten to resurface. Your preparedness and the systems you put in place are your safety net, ensuring that you're not just reacting but actively shaping your life with your newfound resilience and autonomy.

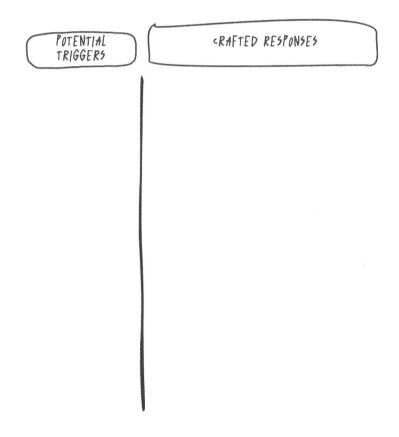

HEARTWORK EXERCISE 13: EMBODY

TIP: Remember, the key to success is preparation. A ready-made response you've mentally rehearsed can make all the difference when old patterns threaten to resurface. Your preparedness and the systems you put in place are your safety net, ensuring that you're not just reacting but actively shaping your life with your newfound resilience and autonomy.

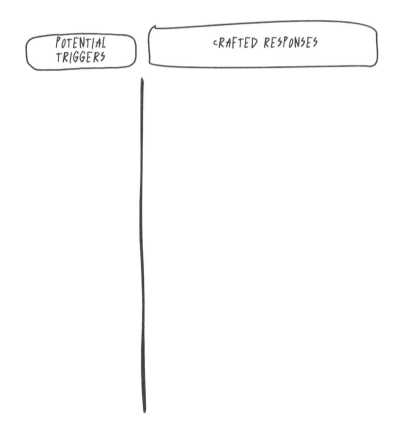

HEARTWORK EXERCISE 13: EMBODY

TIP: Remember, the key to success is preparation. A ready-made response you've mentally rehearsed can make all the difference when old patterns threaten to resurface. Your preparedness and the systems you put in place are your safety net, ensuring that you're not just reacting but actively shaping your life with your newfound resilience and autonomy.

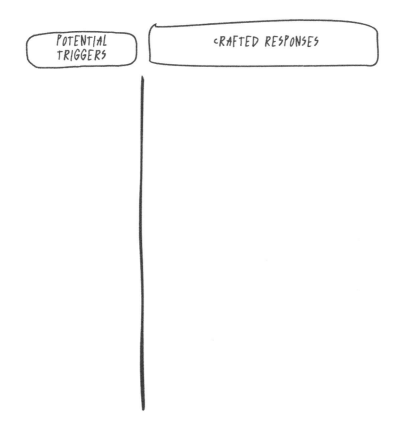

POTENTIAL TRIGGERS

CRAFTED RESPONSES

HEARTWORK EXERCISE 13: EMBODY

TIP: *Remember, the key to success is preparation. A ready-made response you've mentally rehearsed can make all the difference when old patterns threaten to resurface. Your preparedness and the systems you put in place are your safety net, ensuring that you're not just reacting but actively shaping your life with your newfound resilience and autonomy.*

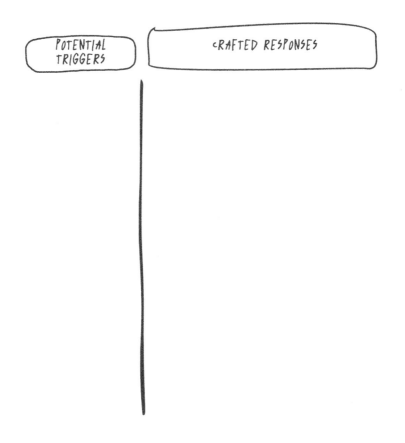

HEARTWORK EXERCISE 13: EMBODY

TIP: Remember, the key to success is preparation. A ready-made response you've mentally rehearsed can make all the difference when old patterns threaten to resurface. Your preparedness and the systems you put in place are your safety net, ensuring that you're not just reacting but actively shaping your life with your newfound resilience and autonomy.

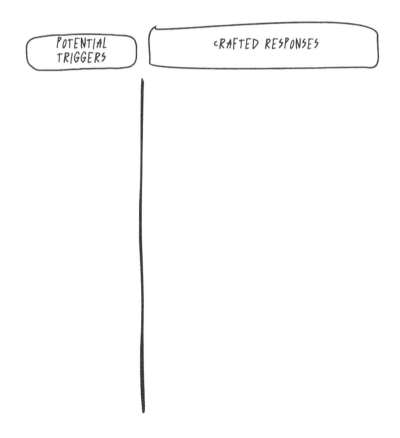

HEARTWORK EXERCISE 13: EMBODY

TIP: Remember, the key to success is preparation. A ready-made response you've mentally rehearsed can make all the difference when old patterns threaten to resurface. Your preparedness and the systems you put in place are your safety net, ensuring that you're not just reacting but actively shaping your life with your newfound resilience and autonomy.

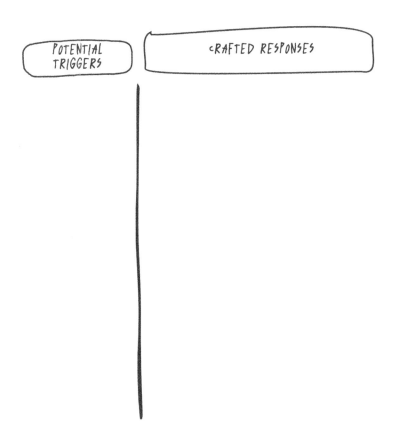

CHAPTER 11

BUTTERFLY SEASON

As we close the pages of the Butterfly SZN guided journal, it's time to reflect on your transformation. Through heartwork, you've learned how to transmute the suffering of your Cocoon Season into the empowerment of your Butterfly Season. You have journeyed all the way from the unawareness of Caterpillar Season, through the unlearning and relearning of Cocoon Season, and into the empowerment and action of Butterfly Season. It's time to celebrate.

Please remember that while you've reached a significant milestone, the journey to maintain and call in the life you want continues. Stay committed. Within your commitment, the true essence of living a Butterfly Season unfolds and reveals the fruits of your transformation.

This book, your companion through your cycles of growth and change, will always be a valuable resource. Life is cyclical, and there may come times when you find yourself revisiting these pages. When you do, know you are taking a proactive measure in your ongoing journey through life's complexities. Picking up this book again isn't about revisiting the past; it's about ensuring you continuously move forward.

Throughout your journey, you've mirrored the Heartwork Exercises with the life cycle of a plant, drawing inspiration from the natural world to illustrate your processes of growth and renewal. You did that while anchoring in the phases a caterpillar goes through to become a butterfly. The theme of change, like flowers and butterflies going through their seasons of transformation, is necessary for your growth.

Completing this journal and the symbiotic relationship between a butterfly and a flower is a masterclass in interdependence and balance. Butterflies pollinate flowers, sparking the creation of new life and spreading more flowers across the garden. Every time a butterfly visits a flower, it feeds itself and helps the flower reproduce and spread, contributing to the overall ecosystem.

That natural partnership illustrates a profound truth about our human existence and transformation. Like the butterfly's crucial role in the life cycle, your experiences, lessons learned, and the changes you've embraced inspire and nurture growth in others. By sharing your story, insights, and perhaps even this journal, you become part of a larger life cycle, contributing to the collective growth. Here's to the endless cycles of transformation, the flowers yet to bloom, and the new journeys that await.

Thank you for using this journal as part of your journey. May your path ahead be filled with growth, joy, and the vibrant colors of your butterfly season.

THE END.

NOTES

NOTES

NOTES

NOTES

NOTES

NOTES

NOTES

NOTES

NOTES

NOTES

NOTES

JOIN THE MOVEMENT, BE THE CHANGE.

When you pick up the Butterfly SZN journal, you're not just buying a book; you're fueling a dream that goes way beyond us. You're supporting a collective healing.

Got a moment from your Butterfly SZN journey you wanna share? Post it on TikTok or Instagram, and we'll hook you up with **25% off your next purchase.**

Just DM @itsbutterflyszn us or shoot over an email to info@butterflyszn. com with your post link, and let's keep this high vibe spreading. Your story is a big part of this bigger picture we're all painting.

Made in the USA
Las Vegas, NV
26 December 2024

15406707R00144